Georgiana Baucus

In Journeyings Oft

A Sketch of the Life and Travels of Mary C. Nind

Georgiana Baucus

In Journeyings Oft
A Sketch of the Life and Travels of Mary C. Nind

ISBN/EAN: 9783744794473

Printed in Europe, USA, Canada, Australia, Japan

Cover: Foto ©Thomas Meinert / pixelio.de

More available books at **www.hansebooks.com**

IN JOURNEYINGS OFT.

A Sketch of the Life and Travels

OF

MARY C. NIND.

BY

GEORGIANA BAUCUS.

CINCINNATI: CURTS & JENNINGS.
NEW YORK: EATON & MAINS.
1897.

INTRODUCTION.

IN the spring of 1894 the duty was assigned me of making the customary visitation of our missions in Eastern Asia. The first episcopal visit to this part of the mission world under the care of the Methodist Episcopal Church was made by Bishop Kingsley in 1869. As this was some years before the planting of our mission in Japan, and Korea was at the time inaccessible, his supervision was restricted to our comparatively new but promising mission in China.

Since then the field occupied by our Church has greatly expanded, embracing now large portions of both the continental and insular empires, with a considerable part of the Korean peninsula.

After my wife had concluded to make the journey with me, it was thought by us both that if "Cousin Mary" could be induced to accompany us, our equipment for usefulness would be largely increased. We were greatly delighted when, after much thought and prayer over the unexpected proposal, she consented to do so. While we coveted her companionship in our prospective journeyings, we were still more eager that she should visit these fields in the interest of the work itself.

The work maintained by the Woman's Foreign Missionary Society in Eastern Asia has reached a magnitude which few are aware of. The occasional visit of some one especially fitted by long experience in the Managing Board in the home-land, joined to a profound and lively interest in the work itself, is warmly welcomed by the missionaries in the field, and can not fail to prove an incalculable benefit.

This volume gives abundant proof of the untiring diligence and unstinted devotion with which this unofficial representative of the Executive Committee sought out every possible avenue of usefulness in her wide journeyings through these pagan lands. Nor does it fail to express the grateful appreciation of her labors felt by all the missionaries in the fields she visited. Her genuine interest in the work, as well as her godly example and singularly wise counsels, made an abiding impression both on the missionaries and the native Christians.

I gratefully acknowledge my personal obligations to Mrs. Nind for valuable aid in many ways, and especially for important information and suggestions relating to the work of the Woman's Society.

We were glad that she found it practicable to tarry in the home of her son-in-law, the Rev. W. H. Lacy, of the Foochow Mission, and return at length by way of Malaysia and India.

This brief memorial of our sister's life, and especially of her visit to the Orient, is from the pen of one admirably fitted in every way for the task. I trust it will be welcomed by a wide circle of readers, stimulating them to a stronger faith and a more self-sacrificing zeal in the cause of the world's evangelization.

W. X. NINDE.

CONTENTS.

CHAPTER I.

CHAPTER II.

CHAPTER III.

CHAPTER IV.

CHAPTER V.

CHAPTER X.

c

CHAPTER XV.

CHAPTER XVI.

INDEX OF ILLUSTRATIONS.

CHAPTER I.

IT was sundown in a country-house near London. The little five-year-old of the family had said her evening prayer as usual, and been put to bed. She was not yet asleep, however, but lay for a long time pondering her first new, wonderful thoughts of God. At last, obeying a sudden impulse, she jumped out of bed, and knelt once more to thank him for her good home and many kind friends. Then, after a little pause, she reverently added, "Please give me a new heart, and make me your good little girl." At this, a sweet feeling of peace and joy stole over her, and, lying down again, she was soon fast asleep.

In the morning a new life began for this little girl, so early led to know and love God; and while she played and romped like other children by the lake and in the garden, and dearly loved, like them, to exchange her pennies for sweets at the nearest shop, there was always a warm feeling in her heart toward God, and a desire to please him, even in her play. On Sundays she delighted in going to Church, and at those times, seated in a high pew by her mother's side, listened intently to all the minister said about the God she loved. She wished, O so much, that she were a boy, and then she, too, might become a preacher. Often, to please the child, her mother turned her pinafore into a gown, and a box into a pulpit, and told her to repeat what the minister had said. Her memory alway served her well, and "first," "secondly," even to "lastly," the sermon was heard again from her childish lips. It came to be the family custom to appeal to Mary, if any part of the sermon was to be recalled. One day a chance visitor wished to refer to a certain head in the sermon of the previous Sabbath. Poor Mary was sound asleep, and her sister had to shake her well to make her know what was wanted of her. Rubbing her eyes, she began reciting the heads in order until the right one was reached; then was down on her pillow again, fast asleep.

It was not until she was twelve years old that she preached her first original sermon. She had been tending day-school, but was soon to enter a boarding-school; and as she thought of leaving her little mates, her heart was full of concern for their eternal welfare. Obtaining permission to speak to them during the rest-hour, she began from the text, "Repent ye." Her sermon had three heads: First, "The meaning of repentance;" secondly, "Why we should repent;" thirdly, "When we should repent." By the time she came to the last head, she had grown so earnest and convincing that her little hearers, already overburdened at the sense of parting, could bear no more, but burst into tears, and, one and all, continued weeping through the rest of the sermon. With such effective preaching in her childhood days, it was not strange that even so great a man as Edward Eggleston should say of Mary in later years, "There is a woman who should be licensed to preach."

But long before Edward Eggleston's days, Mary's mother must have realized the gift that had been bestowed upon her child; for, often when she gave her tracts to distribute, she would add, "And, if you like, you can say a word of exhortation, too." Sometimes the mother put an empty basket in her hand, and she and her sister went out to collect penny offerings for missions. They were taught to save even bones and rags, to pick up pins, and to practice every possible economy for the Lord's work. Once they had a pastor who was, also, a returned missionary from Madagascar. He had left his work only because of extreme persecution instigated by the queen toward Christians, and was biding his time, no doubt, to return. His zeal inflamed Mary's, and she resolved to become a missionary. No sooner was this resolution made than she confided it to her mother--her mother, who was such a lover of missions, who had taught Mary to love them, to save her pennies, and to collect money from others for them. Surely, her mother was the one of all others to tell, the one to be most interested, most glad. Without hesitation, her heart bounding with joy in her new-made consecration, she unfolded her desires. To her dismay, this lover of missions was not pleased to make a missionary of her own daughter. "I can not spare you," she said. "You are too useful, too much needed at home." Neither tears nor remonstrances were of any avail, but only obedience. As Mary yielded, however, with all the strength of her disappointment, she made another resolve. The new resolution was a solemn covenant with the Lord that, if he should ever give her children and all of them should want to become missionaries, she would freely give her consent. In after years she was obliged to keep this covenant in bidding good-bye to a son bound for South America, and a daughter for China.

But it was true, as Mary's mother had said, that the family needed her help. A place was found for her as saleswoman in a shop at some distance from home. She was obliged to board with her employer in rooms over the shop, and became so homesick that she feared she could not keep her trial engagement of one month. But a Sunday-school class, which she began to teach, absorbed her leisure hours, and she soon had no time for homesickness. Doing with her might what her hands found to do, she became so valuable a saleswoman that her employer, fearful of losing her, often advanced her wages; and as a Sunday-school worker she frequently rejoiced over new souls brought to Christ. During this period she was laid low with cholera, and prepared for immediate translation to her heavenly home. Her preparations included the selection of a funeral text, one that has been characteristic of her whole busy life.

"I must work the works of Him that sent me, while it is day; the night cometh, when no man can work."

But night had not yet come to Mary. There were many works still waiting for her to do.

She was now growing up into attractive young womanhood, and suitors began to flock about her. There was one David, who found great favor in her eyes; and as she told her mother of all her lovers, she told her, also, how this David had won her heart. But he did not win the mother's heart, for he was frail, had inherited a weak constitution; and she would not consent to Mary's union with him. Then Mary was filled with grief, and spent many a night in weeping for the lover she could not have. About this time another of her lovers sailed to America, to seek his fortune in that new country. Before leaving, he asked if he might write to Mary. She consented to the correspondence as with a friend, not lover, faithfully showing every letter to her mother for her approval. Finally, a letter came which required very special attention. The mother approved, the father likewise. But the final decision must rest with Mary. What should she do? She could not assume the responsibility alone;

but, for a whole month, by day and night, she prayed for guidance. At last, James Nind, at work in far-away America, received the news that the bride of his choice should be his. But her parents would not permit her to go all the way to America alone; as he had proposed. He must take the long journey to England for her. This would be a great drain on his slender purse; but what will not a man do for the woman he loves? He engaged steerage passage that he might have the more money for the return trip, and joyfully crossed the sea to obtain his bride.

And what will a woman not do for the man who loves her? She left her lucrative position, her loved Sunday-school class, her home, her country, to become the wife of a poor man in a new land.

Soon after their marriage, a grievous disappointment came to her. James came in one day, and, as was his wont, offered to kiss his wife. She drew back in evident dismay.

"What is the matter?" said he.

"I have broken my vow."

"What vow?"

"I solemnly vowed that I would never marry a man who smoked."

"But do I smoke? It is only once in a great while that I take a little whiff."

"That's smoking; and I said I would not marry a man that smoked. I can not undo that; but I certainly shall never kiss a man that smokes."

The reply was too firm to admit of protest, and

James was not like the seaman who remarked: " My wife does not like tobacco. She 'll not kiss me when I smoke; so, when I am in port, I have to give it up."

James was always in port. There were no long voyages to give him opportunity to indulge his tastes. His self-denial must be absolute. Still he did not for a moment think it too great to make for the kisses of her whom he loved best; but wished, no doubt, as he made it, that he could as easily dissipate all the trials which marriage had in store for her. Try as he might, however, his love must impose some hardships which he could only help to bear. He was poor, and his first business ventures ended in such utter failure as to lay a heavy burden of debt on the newly-married couple. They were too honorable to avail themselves of the bankrupt law; but struggled along as best they could under their heavy load. Working hard and saving carefully, it yet required ten or twelve years of constant effort and sacrifice to make them free.

Then it was that the Nation itself began to tremble under a far more terrible load. The most diligent effort and the wisest planning did not suffice to free her. But, in the midst, she was suddenly plunged into all the horrors and atrocities of a great internal war.

Mr. Nind was not drafted; but the cry of freedom so stirred his heart that he felt impelled to enlist as a volunteer.

"What do you think," said he to his wife, "of my going to the war?" What did she think? What would any woman think, with a family of little children about her and no way of providing them with bread? It was with a sinking heart and flagging courage that she replied: "If it be the Lord's will for you, you must go. But let us talk with your mother first, and leave the decision with her." The mother lived not many miles away, but anxiety made the short drive long. All the way they said little, but occupied themselves with prayer and earnest thought. Both felt, rather than knew, what was coming. As they anticipated, the elder Mrs. Nind did not hesitate to reply: "You have a duty to your home and you have a duty to your country. But this is the hour of your country's need."

Mr. Nind's pay, as a private soldier, was thirteen dollars a month, which he used scarcely at all for himself, but rigidly economized, that he might send the most of it to his family. But, at the best, how little it was to feed and clothe a wife and five children! No wonder Mrs. Nind's faith wavered at thought of deducting, as had been their habit, one-tenth regularly for the Lord's work! But she had learned to take counsel, first of her mother, then of her husband's mother; and now, in this difficulty, she appealed to her pastor for advice.

"It does seem hard," he said; "but do n't you think you 'd better trust the Lord a little? Do n't break your covenant with him, unless it proves positively necessary."

Her "little faith" was soon honored by news of her husband's promotion and increase in pay to twenty dollars. From this he was steadily promoted until, at the close of the war, he was receiving one hundred and twenty-five dollars a month and bore the rank of adjutant. Engaging in many battles, he had not once been wounded; and his only illness was an attack of camp-fever. Better than this, he had passed through the various temptations of army life without yielding, and could say to his wife upon his return: "I am just the same as when I left you, Mary."

In harmony with her child-interest in preaching and missions, Mary Clark Nind had always been an earnest temperance advocate, serving at the age of fourteen as president of a juvenile temperance organization. The adding of Nind to her name but added fresh incentive to her zeal; and, amidst all her busy life as a housewife, the care of her home never caused her to forget the necessity of guarding it.

At first she belonged to secret temperance societies, then so much in vogue. But in her integrity of soul and independence of judgment, she saw that the paraphernalia and numerous attendant forms and ceremonies of these societies were but blocking the wheels of progress; so she withdrew that she might give the more vigor and energy to the work itself. The Crusade naturally

attracted her, and she was one of the first to enter
the ranks of the Woman's Christian Temperance
Union.

But her interest and zeal in the cause of temperance were never allowed to run away with her
devotion to other forms of Christian work.   For
thirty-five consecutive years she was a Sabbath-
school teacher.   She had many pupils in that time—
pupils, no doubt, who came to her class in the
same listless, purposeless fashion which is the
habit of a great body of Sabbath-school pupils who
have a Sunday on their hands and do n't know
what to do with it.   But her pupils never came to
a listless, purposeless teacher.   She had an aim, if
they did not; and they were drawn, as by a mag-
net, straight to the Master himself.

With all her directness of purpose, however,
and her success in achieving it, she was wholly dissatisfied with herself.   There seemed to be heights
that she could not compass, joys that forever
mocked her.   For every "up" in her Christian
experience there was a corresponding "down."
Faith ever lacked restfulness; joy, sweetness; and
energy, the quietness and confidence which make
the truest strength.

She wondered if it must always be so; if she
must continue to serve Christ in her weak way;
if she must go on struggling, sometimes conquer-
ing, but often overcome.   She talked with other
Christians about it; but the light that was in them
was no brighter than her own, and her distress

deepened. In the depth of her gloom, she sought out a little, much-despised company of Methodists. There first the light began to break about her, as she listened to living testimonies to Christ's power in saving from every sin and guiding in the way of holiness.

Often she would slip away from the cold formalism of her own Church to enjoy the sunshine of the little Methodist meeting. She felt this to be her true Church-home; and, after counseling with a wise old lady who was aunt to every one in the neighborhood, she asked for a letter from the Church of which she and her husband had long been members.

"Mrs. Mary C. Nind, who has not walked in harmony with our Church for a year, requests a letter to the Methodist Episcopal Church, and is hereby dismissed to you."

The Methodist pastor smiled as he read it, but said that he could receive her upon profession of faith.

At last the rest and peace for which she had longed came into her heart, and with it a greater change in her life than when, in the long ago, she had knelt by her crib to ask God to make her a good little girl. Her children noticed it, and one day she overheard a conversation that startled her:

"Take care! Mother will scold if you do that."

"No, she won't. The *scold* has all gone out of her."

Small wonder that the grace and sweetness of
daily living speedily won them all to the mother's
Master, when, no matter how many Sunday-school
pupils had been saved, they might have been lost
without it?

In her adopted Church she found more of that
freedom of speech for which she had always yearned.
The class-meeting was a weekly delight to her; and
so clear and forcible was her speech, that she was
often called upon to address Sunday-school and
other conventions. Once, upon such an occasion,
her earnest, telling words had no less keen and ob-
servant a listener than Mr. D. L. Moody. Ever on
the lookout for the workers whom the Lord himself had sent into the vineyard, he sought an introduction to Mrs. Nind, and invited her to address
one of his own meetings. Quite overwhelmed, she
could only reply that she must consult her husband
before giving a definite answer.

The consultation brought to her husband's view
much the same kind of a cross as she had to shoulder in 1862. It was his turn now to bide by the
stuff, and permit her to go forth to contend with
the hosts of evil. What a heavy cross it was! He
fully understood its weight now; and all he could
say was to repeat the words that she had uttered
then: "If it be the Lord's will, you must go."

The work of an evangelist compelled her to
give up her Sunday-school class, as well as the quiet
comfort of a home Sabbath, and brought her into
such prominence that she was named, in an editorial

in the *Independent,* as one of two women who should be licensed to preach.

Two other women saw this bravely-expressed editorial sentiment, and carefully noted it for future use. They were workers in the Woman's Foreign Missionary Society of the Methodist Church; and when they came to Winona, Minn., where Mrs. Nind was then living, to organize an auxiliary, they called upon her at once to ask her to become president of the new organization.

The call, like that to many another, seemed inopportune. Family cares were pressing very heavily upon her. There was so much washing and ironing, baking and stewing, sewing and mending, that, ready as she had ever been for every good work, she felt that this must be refused. They did not accept her refusal, but presented the claims of the work again. A second time she refused. A third time they made a glowing appeal. Refusals were growing difficult, but acceptance was more so. There was but one thing left for her to do, and she did that. She burst into tears. The ladies were distressed to see her weep, but were no less persistent. "Tell us all about it," they said; "just everything that hinders you." Then she gave them a full account of all the hard work and various cares that made this new responsibility impossible. They listened with a sympathetic but not in the least defeated manner. Their looks but pre-said what soon fell from their lips: "We can manage that. We shall hire a servant for you, and then

you will have time for this extra work." Thus was
Mary C. Nind installed in her first office in the
Woman's Foreign Missionary Society.

With her hands freer than their wont, she applied herself so zealously to the new undertaking
that the Winona auxiliary was soon known as the
banner auxiliary of the district, and its president
was often in demand to organize auxiliaries on
other charges.

Finally, there came a year when the Program
Committee for the Branch meeting had a serious
discussion. "Who shall give the annual address?"
was the subject under consideration. Some one
suggested the name of the lady who had given the
address at the previous meeting. Another audacious member proposed the name of Mrs. Mary C.
Nind.

"Who is she?" was the first response.

" Did she ever do such a thing?"

" Won't she make an utter failure of it?"

"We know that Mrs. W. can do it, and do it
well. I think we 'd better have her."

But, strange to say, the audacious member won
the day, and it was decided to give the new unknown an opportunity to make a failure. As the
time of the meeting was drawing near, the decision
was sent to her by telegram.

In the not very olden days a telegram entered a
household with much the same explosive effect as
that produced by the bursting of a bomb-shell.
This bomb-shell did not fully burst until the tele-

gram was opened and read. *She* was wanted to deliver the annual address at the coming Branch meeting in St. Louis. She read the words slowly, and handed the telegram to her husband. "I have nothing to wear," were her first words. But there was neither time nor money for a new dress, nor even for a new bonnet. The short, brown dress, which had been her best so long that it was hardly in accord with the prevailing style; the plain, old-fashioned bonnet, which had served her through many a summer,—these had to be taken from the press, where they were as carefully hung and bandboxed as though in the latest fashion and made for this particular occasion; and very hastily she made the only preparations possible for her journey.

She was to be entertained at the home of the grandest lady in the Church. This appalled her quite as much as the responsibility of making the address; for she knew that, in her old-fashioned dress and with her plain domestic ways, she would feel quite out of place in the grand lady's home. So, at her urgent request, she was given a less pretentious place of entertainment.

There was only one day remaining between her and the time of giving her address; and a burden, greater than that of old clothes and fine places of entertainment, settled upon her. Early in the morning she said to her hostess: "If any one calls on me this morning, even if it should be the President of the United States, tell him I am busy and can not see him; and if I am not down to dinner,

do not call me, for I *must* get ready for this evening's meeting."

Shutting herself in her room, she tried to think;
but her thoughts were like obstinate children, refusing to come when most wanted. She knelt in
prayer; but the heavens were like brass above her
head. No thoughts from within, no help from
without, and the meeting coming in the evening!
What should she do? What could she do but
wrestle with the angel, crying in her agony, "I will
not let thee go, except thou bless me?" Suddenly
the blessing came, rushing like a flood into her
soul; and there was her missionary address, hanging like a vivid picture before her mind; beginning, middle, and end, she could see it all. Taking
pencil and paper, she began to write; but her
thoughts flew too fast to be caught and harnessed.
At dinner, which she did not miss, she animatedly
informed her hostess, "I 've got it, and only wish it
were time to begin." That evening, as she rose to
speak, in her short dress and plain poke-bonnet,
there were those in the audience who wondered
among themselves, and even whispered to each
other, "What possessed the Program Committee to
ask her to speak?" The members of the committee who had wanted Mrs. W. said, "I wish we had
insisted upon having her." Even the "audacious
member" must have hung her head in confusion,
and thought, "How could I have made such a
mistake!"

But the baptism of the morning—her "missionary baptism," she loves to call it—was upon her still. In clear, forcible language, she presented the picture she had seen, until her hearers saw it too, and were thrilled with as deep a sense as she of the great need of the heathen world and their own responsibility in supplying it. Some of them told her this at the close of the meeting, and one man made quite a speech about the surprise he had felt at hearing such eloquence from the lips of a plain little woman.

From this time there was no hesitation manifested by Program Committees in putting Mary C. Nind's name down for an address; and when the St. Louis or Western Branch of the Woman's Foreign Missionary Society was divided, she was made corresponding secretary of the part to be known as the Minneapolis Branch. In this capacity she began to travel almost constantly; going to one place to stimulate an old auxiliary, to another to form a new one, to another to address a missionary mass-meeting. To most places the request for her coming was worded to include the Sabbath, and she would be invited into the pulpit to conduct an evangelistic service. Thus were her early ambitions gratified, for she had become both preacher and missionary.

In the midst of these active labors and frequent journeyings a shadow fell athwart her household. Over him whose heart had ever been in her keeping, who had faithfully taken his turn in watching and waiting by the fireside, who never called it self-

denial when it was for her,—over him the shadow
had fallen. "Softening of the brain," the doctor
pronounced it. "He will probably live in this condition for years, though he may die quickly. Nothing else is possible."

Then, through a glass darkly, she looked at the
coming years—her busy life cut off with a snap, many
an opening avenue of usefulness forever closed to
her—and she became the lonely watcher by the side
of one bound, mind and body, by a disease worse
than death. She shuddered, and begged the Lord
to be merciful. He was! The doctor's possible
prediction was verified, and the bound body was
laid to rest; while every one spoke in love and admiration of the freed soul. "He never did a mean
thing in his life," was the testimony of his eldest
son; and the preacher used for his text, "Walk
about Zion, go round about her, tell the towers
thereof."

CHAPTER II.

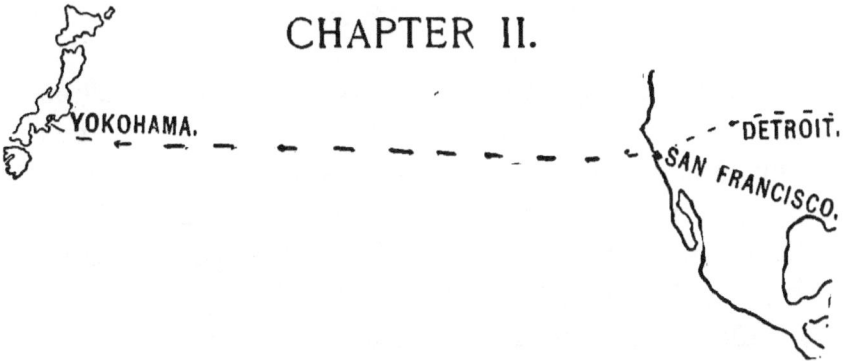

WHEN the General Conference of the Methodist Church met in New York in May, 1888, for its quadrennial session, everybody was expecting a sensation, and nobody was disappointed. Five women had been elected as lay delegates, but neither the women nor the electors knew that they were eligible to election. The Conference itself had to confess to like ignorance; and after directing all of its brilliant lights to an exciting but fruitless search for the needful knowledge, the women were ejected.

One of the ejected women was Mary C. Nind; another was Frances Willard, of the Woman's Christian Temperance Union. Mrs. Nind was on her way to another General Conference, to which she was a *bona fide* delegate. This was the General Conference of Missions, convening that year in London. Before sailing, Miss Willard put a set of resolutions in her hands, requesting their presentation before the Temperance Committee of the Conference. They were presented, but the com-

37

mittee absolutely refused to consider them. Then Mrs. Nind, with happy determination, improved her first opportunity of addressing the Conference by producing and reading the rejected resolutions. Consequently, when the Minutes appeared, they were found, as desired, printed in full.

On her return to the States, she went at once to the meeting of the General Executive Committee of her own Missionary Society, convening at Cincinnati, and commenced her sparkling report in the following way:

"At the Conference in New York, they said I was not a minister, which, of course, was true; then they said I was not a layman, and so gave me no seat. In London, they called me a lay delegate and gave me a seat. Now, what do you say that I am?"

At this, the secretary of the Baltimore Branch arose and said, " You are the noblest Roman of them all." Then there was great applause, and Mrs. Nind stood blushing so violently that an onlooker must have thought it had fallen on her cheeks.

But the journeyings were not all to great Conventions. There were still the short ones here and there to stimulate work in her own Branch; then there were longer ones, stretching even to the Pacific States, that the network of this great organization might be spread over the mountains and across the plains, through the cities and in the hamlets, by riverside and seashore, wherever one woman lives who loves the Lord and his appearing.

There were hard night-rides; there were days when food was not convenient; there were people who opposed the work, and opposed it bitterly. Still there was a never-failing source of comfort to make the nights easy and the days glad, to remove, also, opposition from the way. Mrs. Nind knew just how to pray away her trials and difficulties. One time, as she had so often done, she started to organize work in an entirely new locality. The most influential and wealthy woman in the Church did "not believe in missions," and fought the new undertaking, not with sword nor with pen, but something far mightier than either—her tongue. It became impossible to organize, not alone in this woman's Church, but anywhere in the surrounding country. Still Mrs. Nind did not give it up. Her prayers grew in definiteness, and were now directed toward the chief cause of all the difficulty: "O Lord, if it be thy will, cause her opposition to be overcome; or, failing that, remove her from the way."

The woman was present at the next meeting, seemed touched, and at the close, made an offering of twenty-five dollars to the work. But this was only to ease her conscience. The opposition still continued, until a sudden illness, resulting in death, did, literally, as Mrs. Nind had prayed, "remove her from the way."

After this remarkable answer to prayer, some of Mrs. Nind's friends laughingly professed great uneasiness in her presence; for, they said, "If we

do anything to displease you, you may pray us out
of the way too.''

She was not alone an organizer. As a Branch
secretary, she became responsible, at each annual
meeting, for a large sum of money which she
must manage to raise during the year. Her early
training with a basket, collecting penny gifts for
the Lord, came to her aid in this work. There were
still many penny offerings to collect; but the basket
was so much larger now, that many a time she was
obliged to ask for great things. But asking first
of the Lord, she became so successful in this branch
of the work that it was said of her, as of a famous
collector of Church debts: ''Her funeral text should
be, 'And it came to pass that the beggar died also.' ''

Her success in all branches of the work led to
an earnest request from the woman suffragists to
join their ranks; but her only reply was in the
words of Nehemiah: ''I am doing a great work,
so that I can not *come down.*''

Going about here and there, and always speaking for missions, her earnest words not seldom fell
on the ears of Christian young women whose
consecration took on new hues in their light, and
led them to make the ''reasonable sacrifice'' which
she desired. Sometimes they were needed in India, sometimes in China or Japan; but wherever
they were sent, their minds never failed to turn to
her as their ''missionary mother.''

Her own son had already gone to South America, and a daughter was stationed with her husband

in Foochow, China. Many a time, when engaged
in work on the Pacific Coast, her mother-heart
yearned to cross the great waters, and it seemed
as though she must "run over and see Emma."

Loving, appreciative friends thought she ought
to "run over and see Emma," and once a purse
was all but raised to send her. But "times were
hard," and money was sorely needed in the work;
so, with her usual firmness, their desires and hers
were set aside.

Only a year later the subject was broached
again. She was now resting in her own little
home in Detroit, Mich.; but was under engagement for a number of thank-offering services, which,
with birthday and other anniversary offerings, she
had been among the first to utilize.

She was no longer a Branch secretary. She was
growing old, and for some years had kept a friend
under promise to inform her just as soon as she
saw that power was waning and strength growing
weak. If the promise were kept, she would know
when to resign. But growing fearful at the long
delay, she had already established in her place the
friend who had made the promise.

It was a relative, and one holding high position
in the Church, who came to her, and made the second suggestion that she "run over and see Emma."
He was soon to start, with his wife and two sons,
on an episcopal tour to Japan and China. Would
she not go with him to help him in the Conferences, and to be company for his family on the

journey? "How can I?" she replied. "I have
not money enough for such a trip; I am not young
and strong any more; I have many engagements
to fulfill; and I can not leave my home so long."

But there was tugging at her heart the old desire to see, not only her daughter Emma, but all
of her missionary daughters, and to behold in the
flesh the mission work which she had loved, and
for which she had toiled her life long. She arrayed
her objections in order:

First: "I have not money enough for such a
trip." But children and other friends declared they
would, each and all, be her bankers, before they
would see her lose the trip for this cause.

Second: "I am not young and strong any
more." Calling in her family physician, she received his counsel. "If you are careful of your
general health, and do not drink water without
first boiling it, I see no reason why you should not
take the trip."

Objection No. 3: She could answer this without
consultation; for she knew that, with this journey
in view, all of her engagements could easily be
canceled.

For No. 4, she had to call in the members of
her household, and have a long serious talk with
them, which resulted in the decision that home
cares need not keep her.

The removal of these objections helped not a
little in deciding the, to her, most important
point of all: Was it the Lord's will for her to

go? If so, she knew she could trust Him to supply every need; and in that faith began her preparations for the journey. She had only three weeks
in which to make ready; but long apprenticeship
at traveling had made her feel that she is usually
wisest who takes least.

Only one trunk, and that the size known as
"half" or "hat" trunk; a small hand-bag, and a
shawl-strap! She was not tempted to carry any
fine dresses, for she had none; only plain, sensible
ones, that fold easily; some thick, some thin. Her
shoes were stout, and she carried an extra pair;
her best bonnet, which had already served her
well for ten years, was made modern only by the
addition of a fresh ribbon. All these were put in
her trunk, with her Bible and writing materials.
Her shawl-strap inclosed her shawl, her home-made
steamer rug, and a pair of rubbers; a well-made
English mackintosh was to serve as a traveling
cloak. A strap was fastened to her hand-bag, so
that she could support it from her shoulders; and
in its inside pocket was placed a most important
paper, her doctor's certificate of vaccination.

The last Sabbath before starting came. She
had told few people of her plans; for she dreaded
the influx of callers, which was sure to follow, and
for which she had no time. But feeling too much
like a mother running away unawares from her
children, on the last Sunday she asked permission
to say a few words to the Sunday-school.

The "cloud had arisen," she told them, and

now she was to follow it across the Pacific Ocean, into the dear mission-lands of Japan and China.

That afternoon, as she was enjoying one more Sabbath's quiet with the dear ones at home, the door-bell rang, and a letter was handed in. Opening it, she found inclosed a check for fifty dollars, signed by one of the members of the Church.

On the first day of May, 1894, as many a little girl in Detroit, and out of it, was busy filling dainty little baskets with flowers, a different kind of May-basket was being prepared in the Nind home. This was large and strong, and was filled with sandwiches, and cakes, and fruit enough to last through the five days' journey across the continent.

Long before train time, friends began to gather at the depot. Upon the arrival of Mrs. Nind with her cousin-bishop and his family, they were all permitted to pass the gates, and the great company stood by the train singing "Blest be the tie that binds" to those who were going forth, not to sever any ties, but to make stronger and more blessed the tie that binds the world together.

At Chicago they were joined by two outgoing missionaries; and, though their train left at midnight, another company was in waiting to say good-bye. This time the great depot echoed with the sound of prayer, which must have fallen strangely, in the hush of the night, on the ears of other travelers.

Not all of our travelers had provided themselves with lunch-baskets; but had rather thought it wise to take advantage of the hot meals served in dining and buffet cars. They were like a family party; and not alone by her nephews, but by others as well, was Mrs. Nind often addressed as Aunt Mary. These younger members of the party were greatly distressed because Aunt Mary persisted in remaining by her lunch-basket, and tried again and again to take her into the dining-car with them. Once only they were successful in their efforts, and this time under pretext of its being a birthday party, and so incomplete without her.

Upon their arrival in San Francisco they were snapped up, as if they themselves were new and specially toothsome morsels, by a waiting host of committees; and they were assigned to sermons, addresses, and a big farewell reception, before the dust even of travel had been removed. The fatigue of the journey had less chance still; consequently, when the day came for sailing, one of the party was too ill to go.

It was an unpleasant situation. They were expected in Japan by that steamer, and there was no way of sending word ahead except by expensive cablegram.

The party divided; the missionaries going on, while the bishop and his family remained behind with poor, sick "Aunt Mary." Did it look then as though she had made a mistake; that the doctor had given hasty, unreliable counsel; that she had substituted her eagerness to go for the Lord's will in sending her? She thought it all over carefully,

even anxiously; and concluded she had made a
mistake, not in believing it to be the Lord's will
to send her to Japan and China, but in essaying to
do so much work at the end of a long, fatiguing
journey. "This is a lesson to me," she said. "I
must heed it, and endeavor to *stop this side dan-
ger-line.*"

The hours of pain and suffering were brightened by the kind attentions of many friends.
With their flowers on her table, and earnest words
of prayer in her heart, the days sped until she was
quite well, and another steamer was ready to sail.

A voyage across the Pacific is memorable, if in
no other way, for its length. To those accustomed
to cross the Atlantic in seven days, seventeen
days, without sight, even, of other sails, and with
a short list of passengers, mostly sea-sick, are not
soon to be forgotten; for they form the most "out
of the world," thoroughly blank portion of many
people's entire existence: like a dreary sickness,
which separates one, for days and weeks, from all
that concerns other people, and confines thought
and feeling to the smallest possible compass—that
which concerns one's self.

The *Rio de Janeiro* was known by the unmistakable depreciative appellation of "a slow boat."
Add to this, unusually rough weather, and it is
no wonder that one member of the Nind party
should exclaim with youthful zeal and determination, "If I ever get off from this ocean, I shall
never get on another."

Two of the seventeen days were pleasant; and once the apparent boundlessness above and below was limited by the outline of another ship against the horizon. But, mostly, the fog-horn blew, robbing them of happy thoughts during the day and comfortable dreams at night; and all the time the old ocean "heaved and dashed and roared" with such fury that "Aunt Mary" found it impossible to make daily entries in her journal. Still, though on the defensive continually, she did not once succumb to sea-sickness. Her Detroit friends were praying for her, she knew; and their prayers seemed like a wonderful life-preserver, warranted to protect her from dangers within the ship as well as from those without.

On the last day of the voyage, as the *Rio* entered the still waters of Tokyo Bay, she grew quite steady, and a corresponding change came over her passengers. Some now made their first appearance on deck, and, lying pallid and thin in long steamer-chairs, had few ideas to interchange other than "I never suffered so in my life," "I thought I should die," "O, the sea is dreadful!" "I wish I didn't have to go back." Others were on the alert, straining eyes and opera-glasses in their efforts to get first glimpses of the fairy-land of their dreams. The steerage-passengers, too, were swarming out; and, mostly Chinese, with a few women and children among them, all dressed in their brightest, gayest colors, they made a picture which vied with the land in attractiveness.

But that land! Did ever trees and grass and shrubbery look so green as when after a long voyage over a stormy sea? It was not enough to say, "It is green." One wanted to shout, "How green, green, green it is!"

Then, when the clouds dispersed, and Fuji's shapely head appeared above a ruff of glorious white, one was satisfied, as with a great feast after a weary fast.

Even the water now held plenty to interest: steamers, men-of-war, and merchant-ships of all nations; Japanese schooners, junks, and sampans without number! One could easily be patient while the health officer went his round of inspection, though the plague in Hong Kong had made him more tedious and thorough than usual; and when the great steamer came to anchor, it was difficult to feel the hurry, manifested by some, to get to shore just as soon as possible.

The steamer was surrounded by a crowd of sampans, whose occupants, with little covering other than their dark skins, were making a frantic effort each to get his own boat nearest; and, failing this, were jumping into one another's boats and clambering over one another's shoulders, bound to get on deck any way. In their nakedness and dextrous movements, they looked more like monkeys than men; and one poor missionary, filled with sudden fear, whispered to another, "How are we ever going to teach such people as these?"

As the sampans began to disperse a little, each laden with its own part of the plunder, a larger boat, under the direction of Americans, could be seen approaching. They looked anxiously toward the upper deck and scanned the faces of all who stood there, in their eagerness to know if their friends had come. Less than a fortnight before, they had been out on a similar errand. Without one thought of disappointment, that time, invitations had been issued for a large reception to be given their distinguished guests, and announcements had been made in all the churches of a sermon and baptismal service by the bishop the coming Sabbath. When they went to the ship and found only missionaries, the latter, naturally, missed something from the welcome for which they were waiting. "Mrs. Mary C. Nind was taken sick in San Francisco, and the bishop and his family waited over with her till the next steamer," they hastily explained. The receiving missionaries were very sorry, and told of all the invitations that must be recalled, and the baptismal service to be postponed. "But we are glad to see fresh workers. Welcome to Japan!" they added.

They had recovered themselves, and were now so cordial and kind that the one new worker, who had found it very hard to leave her traveling companions in San Francisco and come on ahead to be a herald of disappointment, soon found it quite as hard to disengage herself from their hospitable entreaties and continue her journey to her appointed

station in the North. But no one is ever more
strongly upheld by a sense of duty than a missionary under her first appointment; so the first
steamer out from Yokohama northward bore, perhaps, the loneliest, most homesick passenger that
ever traversed Japanese coasts. The ship was
manned by a Japanese crew, even to the captain;
not one person on board to whom she could say a
word of English, and their jargon, of course, it was
impossible for her to understand. Once, when the
ship came to anchor in a port *en route*, the shouts
and general noise attendant upon the lading and
unlading of freight so terrified her that she shut
herself in her cabin, not daring to venture outside
until all was quiet again.

"Aunt Mary" was not the only one who had
acquired wisdom through her illness in San Francisco. The missionaries in Tokyo and Yokohama
had not made the mistake this time of planning for
their friends before their arrival. Still there was
no lack of hospitality in their reception. Jinrikishas in plenty were at hand, and, tucked in with
much hand-baggage stowed about them, they were
rapidly and, like every newcomer, laughingly
drawn along the Bund and through several business streets, to be pushed at last up a steep hill; for
they were to be domiciled in mission homes on the
Bluff.

CHAPTER III.

o *FUJI*

o *NAGOYA.*

o *YOKOHAMA.*

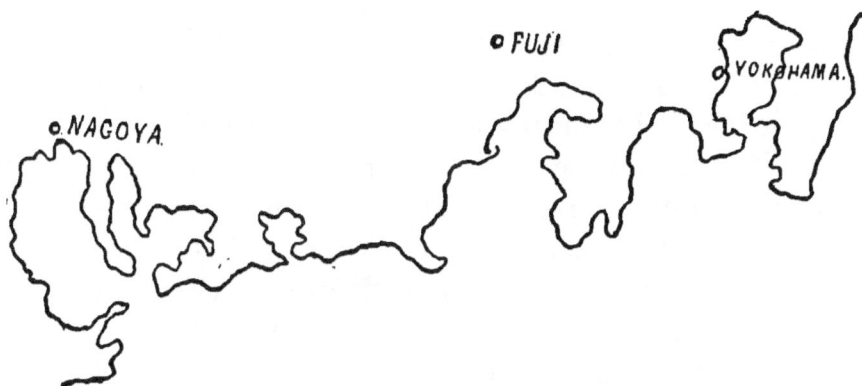

"THIS looks pretty grand," she thought, as she glanced at the high walls and noted the spacious rooms in the home where she was entertained. "How much larger and finer it is than my little home in Detroit!" But "Aunt Mary" wisely said nothing. She had often heard missionaries criticised for the luxury and expensiveness of their living, and now she was to see for herself!

Invitations were soon issued for the postponed reception, and, at No. 13, Tsukiji, Tokyo, the Nind travelers met and addressed a large company of missionaries and Japanese Christians. Upon hearing "Aunt Mary," the latter wondered greatly, expressing their surprise in the words, "*She is so strong.*"

Children's-day was just at hand; and, in almost every church in Japan, committees were on the alert to make it a success. Classes had been taught to recite long passages of Scripture in con-

51

cert, and now must be trained to go on the platform in order, and bow all together, if such a thing were possible, at beginning and close of the recitation.

There were class songs, too, where much the same drilling was required. Speeches, written by teachers, had been memorized by small boys, who were sure to deliver them with great fervency and gusto. Larger boys wrote compositions, which they were taught slowly to unfold before the audience, and, after reading, as slowly refold before taking their seats. All the children had been requested to bring something for a collection; but lest they should think it much giving and nothing receiving, the benevolent teachers had selected their prettiest cards for distribution that day.

But the best part of the preparations there, as everywhere for Children's-day, consisted in the decorations. What quaint mottoes they made of beans, cakes, fruits, even of black, ugly charcoal! How tasteful their arrangement of flowers ! Their beauty was not destroyed by pressing them into stiff, unnatural forms ; but each one, set on its own native branch, drew moisture from a simple bamboo vase, which was fastened, now by a window, then by a door, until a plain, bare church became transformed into a bower of beauty, an apparently living, growing garden. If " Aunt Mary " could have attended every church in Japan that kept Children's-day, she would have seen in all much the same things to enjoy, and would have heard about the same things that she could not understand.

Not being able to compare, she pronounced the one she did attend in Yokohama, most excellent of all, because, forsooth, a woman presided. This woman was the gifted wife of Mr. Ninomiya, who had served his church as lay delegate to General Conference.

June not only brings Children's-day, but, throughout America, it is known as Commencement-month. The Japanese wisely give their annual examinations and confer diplomas in the spring. But missionaries are slow to adopt in their schools the ways of schools about them, even though they may be better; so it happened that a great many invitations to Commencement exercises came flooding in upon the new arrivals. The Girls' School at Nagoya closed early, giving them ample time to return to the later ones in Tokyo and Yokohama; so the ladies ventured to accept that invitation first.

It is an all-day's journey from Yokohama to Nagoya; but one of which even an old resident does not tire, and how much less a stranger! To the latter everything is interesting: the narrow coach, with long cushioned seats at either side and a short one across one end; the funny little three-cornered toilet-room at the other end (for this is an English compartment car and opens at the sides); the passengers with their blankets, *kori*, and smaller bundles tied in *furoshiki*. The Japanese, though very fond of their railroads, do not as yet seem to belong to them. Dressed in English uniform, they make most courteous, faithful officials; but as passengers, bareheaded, with towels twisted about their necks, skirts dangling at their ankles, and clogs on their feet, they look out of place rushing along a station platform or boarding a train. Inside the car, they can make themselves comfortable only by spreading a blanket on the seat and sitting on it, with feet drawn under them, as if it were their own *tatami* at home. At all the larger stations, the shrill, but not loud, cries of "Cha!" "Bento!" can be heard; and passengers exchange a few coppers for a nice pot of hot tea, and a few more for a box of freshly-cooked rice, with chopsticks attached. Sometimes another box goes with this, filled with fish and other condiments; and if the *bento* consists of only one box, an end is partitioned off for the condiments. At one place on this road, one can buy very nice *sushi*, in which the rice is prepared with lobster and many other good things.

The Japanese do not have regular hours for eating, but buy their *bento* when they can, and eat when they get hungry. The *cha* (tea) they drink all along the way, getting a fresh pot as soon as one is empty.

The *seyojin* (foreigner) may tire of these things; but there is one sight on the road of which he never grows weary. If it be a clear day, Fujiyama comes quite near, so near that she seems no longer a cold, ethereal visitant, but a warm, close, real friend. There is her standing-place, down among sunny rice-fields, and looking at her gradual, even slope upward, high aspirations grow, and perfect union between the earthly and the heavenly seems less difficult than before. Sympathy grows, too, with the national love of mountains, and one tries to imagine one's self "only a heathen," with no better god to worship, and many worse.

Nagoya was known to our travelers as the scene of the great earthquake of 1891, which had been described to them so vividly that they had almost felt the shocks and endured the consequent suspense and anxiety experienced, not only here, but throughout the surrounding country. As they alighted at the station, and their jinrikishas were rolling along the smooth, beautiful roads of the city, they unconsciously looked for traces of that disaster. There might be fissures in the ground, or débris of overthrown houses, or, at least, bare, desolate spaces not yet rebuilt. But, to their surprise, only row upon row of neat, well-tiled Japanese buildings passed before them, all bearing an unmistakable air of thrift and prosperity. Many of the homes, with their gardens, were protected from the street by walls, which were often roofed, like the houses, with tiling. High, forbidding gates or doors were the only means of entrance. Before one of these, their jinrikishas stopped. The *Seiryu Jo Gakko!* A high-sounding name, and an imposing entrance! But what did they find inside? A few low, rambling buildings, which, put together, formed the school and home for the missionaries! As they entered the tiny *genka,* utilized as a reception-room, passed across one corner of the tiny next room, used for both study and dining-room, into a tinier room made somehow to inclose a bedroom set, it is safe to say that no one thought, "How grand it is!" Even a short person, without much tiptoeing, could reach the ceiling, and a large person would, too easily, fill the space between wall and bed, and bed and bureau. The little parlor opened on a garden, which never allowed itself to be kissed by the sun, but held the rains in such long embrace that the house was permeated with the moisture.

The school-rooms were small, dark, inconvenient in every way. It had taken two or three together to make a chapel, and the unevenness in the floor was harrowing to a visitor who came upon it unawares.

Within these cramped quarters a girls' school was flourishing; and aside from thinking it a trifle *semai* (narrow, or small), no lack whatever was felt by any of the pupils. They had never seen a finely-lighted, well-ventilated, perfectly-heated school-building. They knew nothing of the apparatus, the specimens, the books considered essential to a well-equipped school in America. Each girl had her own books, the teacher having recourse to a few others, probably from his own little library. There were a few large maps; but geography, like other branches of study, was imprisoned in the ever difficult, incomprehensible Chinese ideograph, and must be freed by most laborious effort, on the part of both teacher and pupil, before one grain of knowledge could be appropriated. Their study, necessarily, was largely a study of signs and characters. When, therefore, they came to their English recitation, and found only twenty-six letters to acquire, it seemed to them like the merest child's play. With astonishing quickness they learned to read. In conversation they were shy, but soon learned to understand. In penmanship and composition they excelled, and took intense delight in penning long, beautiful epistles to their teachers, American friends, and even to their schoolmates.

No matter how *semai* it may be, every girls' school in Japan must have what, alas! is not often found in an otherwise good American school—a sewing-room.

This room has no desks or benches, but is carpeted with soft, thick *tatami* (padded matting), like the rooms of any Japanese home. For long periods, three or four times a week, each class is sent to the sewing-room. There, on their knees, in a semicircle about their teacher, the girls make a low, ceremonial bow. Then they take out their work from the various boxes and bags which they have brought with them. For thimbles they wear, midway on the finger, an indented ring of metal, or sometimes only a band of leather; their skeins of double thread are wound on squares of thin, pretty wood; their needles are short and thick. For their first lessons they practice making even, rapid stitches down the edges of long strips of

cloth. Often, to encourage rapidity, they are
started off together, and the child who reaches the
end first shouts, "Ichi!" (one); the next, "Ni!"
(two); and so on,—the teacher keeping a record
as though it were the first heat of a veritable race.
As.they increase in skill they are allowed to bring
their *jiban* (shirts), and then their *kimono*, until
they learn to make all of their own clothes, and
are able to do a large part of the family sewing in
the school-room, under the teacher's eye.

Often instruction in knitting, crocheting, and
various kinds of fancy work, is interspersed with
the sewing lessons. In the *Seiryu Jo Gakko* many
of the older pupils have become skilled in the art
of flower-making. On Commencement-day, with
their examination papers and fine specimens of
character painting (Japanese writing, but properly
called painting because done with a brush) and
drawing, there were exhibited to visitors delicate
flowers, fancy caps, stockings, mittens, and neatly-
folded clothing, made in the sewing-room. This
exhibition interested our travelers quite as much
as the exercises, which, though novel in arrangement, were formal and tedious. The guests were
seated opposite the pupils. When one was called
upon, she arose, and with slow, measured step
moved forward until, upon reaching the proper
crack in the floor, she halted, bowed, with her
hands in front of her until they reached her knees,
and her body formed a perfect right-angle; bringing herself into position, she drew her *bun* (Jap-

anese composition) from the folds of her capa-
cious sleeve, unfolded it, and proceeded to read in
high-pitched, monotonous tones, which did not
cease till she had read her name and the date of
the performance; still, with the same leisurely air,
the *bun* was refolded, replaced in the sleeve, and
the pupil retired. English compositions, recitations, and songs proved fairly intelligible; but there
were the speeches—speeches to graduates, speeches
to undergraduates, welcome speeches to guests, re-
plies from the guests, including more speeches to
students. By the time the speeches were finished,
even the *seyojin* could appreciate what followed.
The lady teachers and some of the older pupils
withdrew, to return forthwith, bearing great trays
filled with paper packages of cakes, and other trays
containing tiny, saucerless cups of tea, to refresh
tired speakers and weary listeners. There was
much art observed in the serving, the most honored guests being approached first, and with the
finest cakes; then the other guests and the teachers. Of the students, the graduating class were
first waited upon, and with a finer variety than the
others.

The *Sotsugyoshiki* (Commencement exercises)
were succeeded by a *Sobetsukwai* (farewell reception).

One of the missionaries was to return to
America, and no possible stretch of Japanese etiquette would admit of her leaving without a proper
farewell reception. Parting presents, too, came in

such numbers, and even bulk, that it was difficult
to find places for them either in the little home to
be left or in the boxes to be sent.   Some of them
were family heirlooms of great value and antiquity,
each bearing so distinct a character that duplicates
were impossible.   Little wonder that a missionary,
fresh from her *Sobetsukwai*, should say to a tourist,
"If you want really fine souvenirs of Japan, just
stay and teach long enough to have a *Sobetsukwai!*"

Not alone was the returning missionary thus
generously treated—her guests also were made re-
cipients of many favors, among which were well-
executed specimens of the school-girls' own handi-
work.   Enriched by these, and more by glimpses
given with them of great possibilities of love and
loyalty and sacrifice, beneath an apparently unruf-
fled, formal exterior, they returned to Yokohama.
In the long life that had gone before, the books on
missions, the correspondence with missionaries,
their addresses,—nothing had brought Aunt Mary
so near the heart of the Orient, in such close touch
with the real life and work of the missionary, as
the few days in Nagoya.   She felt as though she
had been trying to climb a mountain; but slowly
plodding at its base, suddenly she had come upon
a tramway, and been carried swiftly to the top.
How changed everything was!   Slopes that had
seemed gentle and easy from below, were now
found to be jagged and rough; and in places that
had looked steep, level swards, making delightful
resting-places, were discovered.   How could she

make others see what had now become clear to her! How could they from below understand the things above!

That night in Yokohama the rapid ringing of bells, suggesting a fire, brought her quickly to the window. Looking down, she saw rows of swinging, swaying lanterns, all converging in a cloud of thick, black smoke. Soon a bright blaze burst forth, and she could see that they were carried by men, who were running to the fire from all directions. The firemen were out, too, with engine and hose-cart; but what could they do with the pretty bon-fire of paper and straw! The best work was done with hooks and ladders, tearing down surrounding buildings. In this way the fire was checked, but not until five thousand people had been compelled to tie their belongings in blankets and go forth to seek shelter in the home of some relative or friend. The next morning in the smoldering ashes of their homes, little was to be found, other than broken tiles and a few charred *godown* (fire-proof store-houses); but with ready spirits, like a boy whose play-house has fallen, they hastened to clear the ground and erect anew their tiny homes of wood and paper and straw.

After the fire, an earthquake! It was only a few days later. Aunt Mary was in Tokyo, at No. 13 Tsu-kiji, where the reception had been given. Busy in her room, preparing for a women's meeting, all at once she heard a heavy sound like a peal of thunder. The floor began to upheave and roll as if at sea.

She arose and started to leave her room, hitting her knee against a falling chair and table as she went. Reaching the hall, she met the others in the house coming from their rooms. She was the first to speak: "What is to be done? Shall we stay here, or go down stairs?" Her hostess falteringly replied: "I hardly know. Suppose we go below?" As they started, the chimney in the room just vacated by Aunt Mary, fell with a crash through the floor into the dining-room beneath. They proceeded down the swaying stairs to meet another shock at the foot, and some policemen coming into the hall to inquire if any one had been killed, and if they could be of service.

This was the end of the earthquake! Just a few throes of old Mother Earth, and the blocks of brick and slabs of wood, which her children had set up, were toppled over. Thousands of dollars' worth of property destroyed in a moment! Lives endangered, more shocks a probability! A terrible catastrophe, yet it did not break up that women's meeting! Twenty-five women, fully one-half the number expected, came to hear Aunt Mary; and in spite of the earthquake, though, perhaps, more because of it, the meeting was pronounced a great success.

Neither did the earthquake break up a second reception, which had been planned for the following day. This time the guests were all missionaries, about sixty in number, representing many different boards.

CHAPTER IV.

MOST of the temples of Japan are disappointing. They are found, it is true, on every high hill and under every green tree; but the high hills and the green trees are in lonely, isolated spots; some of the temples are memorial shrines, closed except on great anniversary occasions; while others that may be open always are only occasionally visited by worshipers.

The real worship of Japan is largely before the ancestral shrine in the home and the Imperial picture in the school. So it has come to pass that temples are often used for tea-houses, and that any foreigner who pleases can have his photograph taken, sitting on the thumb of *Dai-Butsu* himself.

Incongruous as it seems, a temple convenient to the people, and located in a pretty spot, is often rented for a Christian social; and the songs of praise and words of prayer, which always rise to Jehovah on these occasions, bring not so much as one frown to the faces of ever-smiling Buddhas.

63

But there is one temple in Japan which satisfies the preconceived notion of what a temple should be—the Asakusa Temple in Tokyo. Situated in the heart of the great city, it is easy of access to all classes of people ; and, as it contains a great variety of gods, each worshiper is pretty sure to find the object of his prayers. The long road leading to the temple is lined with shops and booths, presenting a gala appearance, more like a great fair than the entrance to a house of worship. Within the temple inclosure, and even in the temple itself, pigeons are flying about, to be fed by these worshipers, as other pigeons are fed by Mohammedans in the Pigeon Mosque at Constantinople, and by Christians in St. Mark's Square at Venice. The most interesting idols are the travelers' god in the gate, who receives offerings of sandals from those about to start on a journey, and, in the temple, the god of matrimony and the famous pain-god. This latter is always surrounded, and pitiful indeed it is to see the real faith with which its smooth, shining surface is rubbed and re-rubbed to relieve the pain of diseased members. But, after all, it is no more superstitious than carrying a horse-chestnut in one's pocket to relieve rheumatism ; for they can tell of people who rubbed the pain-god and got well, and what other reason can be given for wearing the horse-chestnut?

Of the steady stream of worshipers flowing so constantly in and out of the temple, there are more women than men ; and they seem more earnest in their devotions, often weeping in the intensity of desire, and continuing at length the "vain repetition," for which they think they will be heard; while the men seem satisfied oftentimes with a hasty obeisance only. Before each idol is a money-chest, for no one would think of proffering a request without first making an offering. As with men, so with gods is the thought; each must be bribed to do a favor.

Aunt Mary's jinrikisha runners could not take her too quickly from this, the first heathen temple she had ever visited. How glad she was when they drew her to the building known as the Central Tabernacle, and she could see the place where a Christian worker had tried to cast his net on the right side of the ship, and was earnestly endeavoring to draw in the masses!

After a busy week of Commencement exercises in boarding-schools at Tokyo and Yokahama, there came a quiet Sabbath, closing with the postponed baptismal service by the bishop; and then Conference. This was the Annual Conference of the Methodist Church in Japan, including an auxiliary organization known as the Woman's Conference.

The days had become warm and sultry. The high ceilings and large rooms, that had seemed so grand and spacious, were none too high and large now. Mosquito curtains were carefully drawn about the bed at night; but there was no screen for the day, and neither curtain nor screen could protect from the ubiquitous and attentive flea.

The Mission Compound at Aoyama, where the

Conference was to assemble, was a scene of confusion. Buildings racked by the earthquake had been condemned and were awaiting repairs; chimneys had fallen, rendering other buildings ineffective; men were at work erecting a temporary tabernacle to serve as an assembly hall.

Resident missionaries were going about attending to the entire readjustment of their plans with the calm, quiet manner which is the rightful, though often unclaimed, inheritance of those who "count not their lives dear unto themselves." In the general change, it came about that the Woman's Conference was held in the Harrison Industrial Home, which was new and so well built that it had been comparatively uninjured by the earthquake. This was one of the many buildings that Aunt Mary had seen by faith from afar. How well she remembered the earnest appeals, sent home by a dear, loved missionary, for money to found that institution! Even when that missionary lay ill, and some thought dying, she wrote: "I am willing to die; but it seems to me that a shadow will follow me into the better land if I do not live to see an industrial school in Tokyo." But there was no shadow to follow her now! A bequest of five thousand dollars had made this building possible. A missionary had been inspired to undertake the work, and already applicants for admission had to be turned away.

It was vacation time, though a number belonging to the school had been detained by the illness of one of the pupils, Chicka Hasegawa. One very warm night, O Chika San had become heated and thrown off her heavy *futon* (wadded quilt). Falling asleep, she did not notice that a draft was creeping over the *tatami* and about the *futon* on which she was lying. She awoke with a cold, and was now gasping away her life in a severe attack of pneumonia.

Just below, the Woman's Conference was assembling. Aunt Mary was made president, and performed the duties of her office with promptness and dispatch. At best, it was a wearing, wearying session. The dying lay near; one of the members had been injured at an open-air meeting, and was in the hospital undergoing an operation on her right eye; the earthquake had done so much damage that thousands of dollars would be needed for repairs. But through it all, for an hour every afternoon there hung on one door in the school a card marked " Resting." Aunt Mary was taking her afternoon nap. Once overwork compelled her to enter a sanitarium; and ever since her graduation she had faithfully maintained a post-graduate course. This course consisted of a morning bath, followed by calisthenics; no tea or coffee, but only hot water; a long walk and an hour's rest during the day; and eight hours of sleep at night in a room well aired and ventilated. Methodical and exact in all these particulars, the " sleep account " was kept with special precision; and those who inquired at the breakfast-table how she slept the night before were pretty sure to get a reply like this: "First-rate! I 'm half an hour ahead now;" or "I 'm just even;" though sometimes a very poor night or some exigency of travel would compel her to answer, "I 'm an hour behind," or "I 've two hours to make up."

After Conference, through the intense heat of July and August, every *seyojin* who can, slips away to the mountains or the seashore for a little rest. This year, many of the missionaries were detained, hoping to put their buildings in repair before the opening of school in September. Some took the risk of remaining in houses pronounced unsafe, until plans for rebuilding could be properly prepared by the overworked foreign architect. One missionary, however, was sufficiently disengaged to accompany Aunt Mary to Nikko.

It is quite as unromantic to go to Nikko by rail as to stand in Athens and see a railway train whizzing past the Arch of Hadrian. One can, of course, leave the train at Utsunomiya and take the old jinrikisha road into Nikko. But expedition, not enjoyment, is the watchword of the American traveler; and so she foregoes the quiet, solitary coach, with its quaint gentle steed, in favor of the crowded car and the shrieking engine; denies herself an afternoon alone with the trees and their dancing sunbeams and shadows, to be hurried, as over the plains of a desert, almost to the Imperial shrines themselves. Once in a while she catches a glimpse of the stately avenue she might have traversed, and wonders if, after all, the longest way round were not the best way there. But it is too late now, and she has to content herself with the short ride from the station to her hotel.

The artistic Japanese, whose fondness for Fuji-yama leads him to paint her graceful cone on his *fusuma* (sliding doors), give it the chief place in the ornamentation of his teacup and even of his teakettle, dearly loves Nikko. For Nikko is, as travelers often observe, the embodiment of two glories; one glory of the mountains, the trees, the waterfalls, and another glory of the temples, the shrines, the gateways, the bridges. But as it is only the painted image of Fuji whose beauty is never clouded, it is the Nikko of the imagination alone that is always *kekko** (beautiful). Often the mountains are concealed by mists, the roads are too muddy to travel, and the temple courts seem decorated only with mold and decay.

Aunt Mary remained too short a time to subject Nikko to many tests, visiting only the most accessible places. She failed to count the long row of stone gods which, it is said, no two people have ever counted alike; did not double herself into a *kago* (basket suspended from a pole) to be carried on the shoulders of two or three men over the mountains to Lake Chusenji; did not even stop long before the marvelous Red Bridge, used only

---

*Referring to the proverb, that no one can see "kekko" until he has first seen Nikko.

by the *Tenshisama* (Son of Heaven, the emperor's title), but after a week hastened on to Sendai.

Hakodate was her objective point; but the passport, which she carried, permitted her to break her journey at several places *en route*. It was six o'clock Saturday evening, when she and her missionary friend alighted from the train at Sendai. Before they could pass the gates, or receive the greetings of the lady who had come through to meet them, a trim little policeman had stepped up, put forth his hand, and called out, "*Menjo.*" He was dressed in his summer uniform of white, with a white scarf hanging from his cap to protect him from the sun, and looked cool and comfortable. But they had just got off from the train after a hot summer day's journey, and were warm, dusty, and tired. They had not expected to show their passports here, so had stowed them away in their hand-bags. Aunt Mary, with her usual method, could put her hand upon hers at once. It was produced, examined, and she went on with Mrs. S. to her jinrikisha. But Miss R. did not come. Mrs. S. went back for her and neither of them came. A great crowd gathered around the jinrikisha. They gazed at Aunt Mary's face, at her bonnet, at her gloves, at her hand-bag. They talked about her, gesticulating with their hands. How uncomfortable she was! What could be the cause of the delay? At last the delinquents appeared, with the policeman and a Japanese youth in ordinary dress. The latter was a friend, who had promised to go

to the *keisatsujo* (police station) in Miss R.'s behalf.
Her passport was wrong. It allowed her to go to
Hakodate all right, but not to stop at Sendai; so
she must go on the next train, leaving at two
o'clock in the morning.

But the Japanese friend interceded so well that
at eleven an official appeared at Mrs. S.'s home, to
state that Miss R. could remain.

This caused the tired travelers to send up a
note of thanksgiving and hasten to bed. Scarcely
was the house quiet when another messenger came
to say that, after all, unless Miss R. was sick, they
would be obliged to send her on; but if she could
produce a medical certificate, stating that she was
not able to travel, then they could let her stay.
By this time Miss R. did feel really ill; so a doctor
was called, and two certificates were made out, one
for the chief of police, and another for some one
else, perhaps the mayor of the city or the governor of the *ken*. When this was done, still Miss
R. could not rest; for letters of thanks must be
sent to these magnates for their honorable conde-
scension in permitting her to break her journey
contrary to the provisions of her passport.

It was now four o'clock in the morning. The
mosquitoes were inside the nets; and as soon as
the morning sun had put them to shame it was too
hot to sleep. And so it happened that, to the for-
malities of Japanese passport regulations, must be
charged an enormous debit on Aunt Mary's "sleep-
account."

Hakodate combines the triple attractions of the city, the mountain, and the sea. To be sure, the city has no marble mansions, no hotels with guests in the fourteenth story, no great stores with departments for every variety of goods, from hats to boots. There is never a railway-train whizzing in and out; never a cable-car, to take one swiftly up and down the steep hills; never a restaurant, where one may indulge in a dish of ice-cream; never a soda-fountain. The night is not made like the day, by luminous rows of electric lights. There are no steam-launches and beautiful yachts plying up and down the harbor; there are no fine pavilions and bathing-houses on the beach; no rest-houses or pretty summer hotels on the mountain; none of the common appointments of the city or of the summer resort.

Yet it is a city—a busy, prosperous city—where thousands of most enterprising Japanese, emigrants from the main island, live and work, plan and execute, until it is said of them, as of their forefathers, "Shinde shimaimashita" (dying, finished).

In their enterprise they have taken advantage of convenient mountain springs to plant public waterworks on the hillside, and they have protected their houses from the cold, to some extent, by making the windows and doors in foreign style. They have *Koyenchi* (public gardens), containing a museum; several monumental slabs of unhewn, unpolished stone; and a "Point Lookout," commanding a fine view of the harbor.

At a proper distance from the city is a solitary brick chimney for the dead, a crematory, fairly-well patronized. So much for modern improvements.

As a seaside resort it affords a great variety of bathing; for at one side of the narrow neck of land which makes Hakodate Head a part of Yezo there is almost always a high surf, and the other side, across the harbor, is a broad, gently-sloping beach, covered by water as still as any lake; then, around by the rocks where the mountain droops to meet the sea, are natural swimming-pools of any desired depth.

The mountain is well wooded, containing many ferns and a variety of wild flowers; is only eleven hundred feet above the level of the sea at its highest point—so presents few difficulties of climbing—and is located in such a way as to give charming views of land and sea and sky.

A home on this mountain, in this city by the sea, had been chosen as the best place for Aunt Mary to avoid the heat and recuperate for the hard trip to Korea, which was to come next on the bishop's itinerary.

Rumors of war were in the air. Serious complications in Korean affairs had already led, it was reported, to hostilities between Japanese and Chinese soldiers.

One of the missionaries, resting with Aunt Mary in Hakodate, was the recipient of a Tokyo daily, published in English. It had to come the long railway journey from Tokyo to Aomori, con-

suming the better part of two days and a night;
then another night across the straits, reaching
Hakodate in the morning, usually within three
days of publication.

After breakfast and prayers, it grew to be the
custom for every one to tarry in the sitting-room
for the reading of the paper, especially the part
giving the latest war developments. At last they
read that which they had feared—a formal declara-
tion of war on the part of the Japanese emperor.
It was manly and forceful, not once stooping to
undignified accusation, but apparently actuated
only by a sense of justice and earnest desire to
vindicate the truth. While they trembled at the
temerity of this call to arms with China—great,
old, hoary-headed China—they admired the spirit,
and thought it hardly worthy of defeat.

A few days later another proclamation appeared.

"This can't be the real one. Somebody is
making fun, and imagining what the Chinese emperor will say. Just hear: 'As Japan has violated
the treaties and not observed international laws,
and is now running rampant with her false and
treacherous actions, commencing hostilities herself,
and laying herself open to condemnation by the
various Powers at large, we therefore desire to make
it known to the world that we have always followed
the paths of philanthropy and perfect justice
throughout the whole complications; while the
Wojen (an ancient name for Japanese, expressive
of contempt), on the other hand, have broken all

the laws of nations and treaties, which it passes our patience to bear with. Hence we command Li Hung-Chang to give strict orders to our various armies to hasten with all speed to root the *Wojen* out of their lairs. He is to send successive armies of valiant men to Korea, in order to save the Koreans from the dust of bondage. We also command the Manchu generals, viceroys, and governors of the Maritime Provinces, as well as the commanders-in-chief of the various armies, to prepare for war, and to make every effort to fire on the *Wojen* ships, if they come into our ports, and utterly destroy them. We exhort our generals to refrain from the least laxity in obeying our commands, in order to avoid severe punishment at our hands. Let all know this edict as if addressed to themselves individually. Respect this!' That is only the last of it, but the first is just about as bad," continued the unappreciative reader.

All agreed with her that there must be some mistake—that such a puerile, undignified document could not have emanated from the throne of a mighty empire, representing a great though ancient civilization.

But it proved to be a genuine translation of the original proclamation, and was enough, *per se*, to fill its readers with intense sympathy for the *Wojen*.

Day by day they waited, with increasing eagerness, for the little three-days-old newspaper. But sometimes, though they waited long hours in the

sitting-room, no neatly-uniformed postman appeared at the door, and sometimes he bore other
mail—no paper.   Then, again, there would be two
or three papers, from which they gathered a mea-
ger account of a battle on land—hundreds of Chinese killed, only a few Japanese wounded—or of a
naval encounter, which left several of the enemy's
ships foundered, the Japanese fleet unimpaired.
They wondered whether to accept much, little, or
none at all of these accounts, and longed to read,
with friends across the sea, the telegraphic news in
the New York *Tribune* or the London *Times*, and
know surely what was transpiring in the little
peninsula so near them.

"Is it safe for Aunt Mary to go on to Korea
during these troublous times?" was a question
often debated, but as often left unanswered.

The Japanese everywhere were bracing themselves as for a long, hard struggle.   Even the
Yaso-Shinja (Christian believers), who had been
regarded with disapproval for supposed lack of
patriotism, were not a whit behind Buddhists and
Shintoists in offering large contributions to the
War Fund.   Church-doors flew open, and people
were invited to concerts for the benefit of the Red
Cross Society.

Preachers belonging to the reserve corps of the
army did not go to interior appointments, but, according to military orders, remained in port, ready
to respond to a probable call for more soldiers.

The only Christians who did not rise on the

high tide of popular favor at this time were the Quakers. Conscientiously opposed to war, their ranks suffered terrible depletion; for how could a Japanese remain a Quaker when his country's honor was at stake! Everywhere he went, even to the small hours of the morning, he heard *ikusa no hanashi* (talk about the war). His intensely patriotic mind was inflamed with excitement, and he felt—with every other Japanese man, woman, and child—that the greatest glory of living lay in the possible privilege of dying for his country.

The national and religious festivities in which all were accustomed to engage with such pleasure, were suspended; for how could one rejoice at such a time as this? Besides, they needed the money for the war.

With the exception, however, of a few surface ripples, the intensity of patriotic feeling was concealed from the *seyojin* by the usual decorum and quiet humility prescribed by every rule of Japanese etiquette. The Japanese, even more than the *seyojin*, were without reliable news of the war; but, ever confident of the continued and ultimate success of their country's arms, they felt it to be quite unnecessary and wholly beneath their dignity to indulge in boastful prediction. One, however, in a burst of confidence, exclaimed, "We would every one of us die before we would give up our country to China."

In the Mission Home, with the old question, "Ought Aunt Mary to go to Korea?" other questions arose: "How is the war going to affect our work?" "Shall we be able to open our schools at the usual time?" "Will the girls come?"

But all had to be "laid on the table" as problems that could not yet be solved, and every one devoted her time and thought to rest and recreation. Directly after the noonday meal each day, there was a Bible-reading, conducted by Aunt Mary; then a nap, followed by a walk. In the evening there was music, and very often exercises with bean-bags, "to develop the muscular," as Aunt Mary called it. She proved herself a champion at these exercises, and soon became the popular captain, for her side always won.

One afternoon the walk was made to include a mountain-climb, with supper on the peak. The sun had sunk low enough behind the mountain to throw most of the paths in shadow. There were little climbs, then restful walks on a level; dainty ferns and beautiful flowers were continually attracting some of the party from the path, and they found it difficult to heed the injunction, "Better take those on the way back!" In the deep, deep shade of tall, lonely trees, disturbed only by the hoarse cawing of *carasu* (crows, which are very numerous in Hakodate, and, in fact, all over Japan), as many as could, found a resting-place on a box which covered one of the feeders of the water-works below. On, after a little, up the mountain side, until the ridge was reached, and the sea appeared in little pieces here and there! "From one point on the ridge you can see the water in seven different places," was the information volunteered by an old resident.

But, however charming the bits of views on the way up the mountain, one feels sure that it is more charming at the top, and hastens on. The steepest part came just before they reached the summit, and here one of the party gave out. It was not Aunt Mary, however. Her sixty-eight years seemed to be a spur, not a drag, to her feet; and she was among the first to shout down to the exhausted missionary what a beautiful view she was missing. Beautiful, indeed! Below—it seemed directly under them—was the school and the home they had just left. These buildings were partly hidden by trees; but the French school in front came out in bold relief. A little to the south were the Greek church and the French cathedral; near them, the costly new temple, not yet finished; and, in the *machi* (town) below, the largest temple of the city. They could look into the clear water of the public reservoirs, which seemed almost near enough to reflect their faces; and down upon the Lookout tower in the public gardens. The roofs of the houses presented a curious appearance; not tiled, nor thatched, but shingled, with even rows of stones laid on to keep the shingles down. There was so little room at the base of the mountain that they were crowded close together, and even stretched across the low isthmus, where they appeared in imminent danger of ingulfment in a tidal wave.

The little fishing villages of Shirasawabe and Yamasetamari brought to mention the senior Circle of King's Daughters that had grown up in the school. For years they had divided, and gone faithfully once a week, though often through deep mud and fierce storms, to these villages to teach what they knew of Jesus ; never once hindered, in their loving service, by the insulting words, showers of stones, and barking dogs, which sometimes were their only reward.

But the beauty of the view did not lie in a perfect chart of the city and its outlying villages. There was the calm, quiet, deep-blue harbor, so still that every boat and every sail seemed fixed and motionless; beyond, the sharp, jutting peak of a volcano rose in clear, well-defined outline against the summer sky; across the isthmus, the bright blue sea was shining and dancing in the beautiful, curved beach it had made for itself between the mountains.

The view down the opposite decline of the peak was almost as lovely ; in every direction, charming blue sea and glorious green mountain ; here a bit of sea, there a dash of mountain ; now drawing near in loving embrace, then retiring in blushing timidity. But the sun was sinking rapidly, and the mists were rising, enveloping both mountain and sea in billows of purest white and softest down ; so they hastened to descend, filled with blessed thoughts of Him who "setteth fast the mountains by his strength," and "measureth the waters in the hollow of his hand."

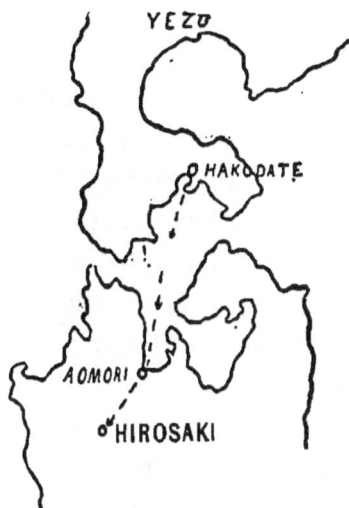

CHAPTER V.

THE favorite summer resort of the Japanese is not the seaside nor the mountain, but the hot springs. The volcanic, oft-quaking islands of Japan abound in springs of hot water, which make natural baths for the people, and have so accustomed them to the use of hot water that they would not only shiver at thought of an Indian shower-bath or an English cold-water plunge—they would consider them wholly lacking in proper, cleansing qualities. Even the lukewarm bath of an American sanitarium would not satisfy, but the water must be heated seven times hotter than it is wont to be heated in any other country. At the almost boiling temperature to which nature delights in heating many of her baths in Japan, her people are satisfied, and feel sufficiently cleansed, heated, luxuriated; for in the winter-time they frequent the public baths of the city quite as much to get warm as to become clean; and in the summer they go to the hot springs of the country to luxuriate. Tea-houses and hotels in these favored spots are often crowded with guests, who leave off lounging in the bath, only to lounge in their rooms awhile, and then return to the bath. The baths often have high

6

81

medicinal qualities, holding sulphur and other minerals in solution.   Such are the baths at Yuno-kawa, only five miles distant from Hakodate.   One or two of the hotels at Yunokawa have conformed to the requirements of modern civilization by the erection of a private bath-room for the convenience of *seyojin*, who so strongly object to entering the public bath, used in common by both sexes.

One afternoon, in place of the customary walk, Aunt Mary and her missionary friends took a drive to Yunokawa.   Jinrikishas were slow and rather expensive; so they engaged a *basha*.   A *basha* is a short omnibus, whose top and side curtains of canvas make it look not unlike an emigrant wagon. It is supposed to be planned for six people; but eight, or even ten, persons are often seen sitting, crowded and uncomfortable enough, on its narrow seats, with their stiff, hard cushions.   It is drawn by horses, who are groomed as poorly as they are fed, and whose harness, once of leather, has been mended with pieces of rope so many times that the original has almost disappeared.   The roads are as poor as the *bashas*.   Torn up by the snows of the winter and the rains of the spring, they are full of ugly holes, into which the *basha* descends with a thud, coming up again with a jerk, which gives the unwary passenger smart raps on head, hands, and feet, and causes the inexperienced *basha* traveler to go through all possible stages of nervous apprehension and fright; for sometimes the *basha* goes down, and does not come up again until every

passenger is lifted out of the end, and the poor
horses are whipped, and pushed, and whipped again,
in the endeavor to get them to pull even the
empty wagon out of the hole. Then, again, the
basha enters a great sea of mud, and its movements become uncertain, like those of a ship in a
storm. It tips, it sways, it goes over! No one
is drowned; but—

The unevenness of the road is very hard on the
basha; and sometimes the pole, or a whiffletree,
snaps in two, making another break in the journey.
Then Japanese ingenuity is brought into play to
rearrange the rope-harness, so that the horses may
be driven tandem.

None of these accidents happened on the way to
Yunokawa, though one missionary, for fear, walked
a part of the way. There was much jolting; but
Aunt Mary endured this patiently, making up, in
the spring and activity of her own vigorous nature, for the springless condition of the carriage.

The hotel with the private bath-room had been
chosen for a resting-place. Pretty housemaids came
to the door with an "Irrashai!" (word of greeting), and a row of heelless slippers for the *seyojin* to
put on after their shoes were removed. Camp-
chairs were brought to their cool, airy room, which
had one whole side open to the breeze; and they
were asked if they would have coffee. This meant
a drink prepared from a curious compound called
coffee-sugar, which is loaf-sugar mixed with what
is supposed to be coffee, and prepared by simply

pouring on hot water. Served in a large cup and saucer, with a pewter spoon, it is considered a special mark of respect to the foreign guest. But all seemed to prefer the well-prepared native drink of clear, straw-colored tea. While some were refreshing themselves with the tea and small cakes resembling English biscuits, others were enjoying a plunge in a hot sulphur bath. As they did so, they thought with pity of the poor little paralytic lady, who had come to Japan as an independent missionary, and had spent whole seasons in this hotel in Yunokawa, finding in the daily bath her one respite from pain.

But far better to Aunt Mary than mountain or sea or hot springs, were the calls from Japanese Christians, the opportunities to preach the new testimonies that she so often heard of the ever-prevailing power of Christ in the salvation of souls. How glad she was to meet a Christian soldier at the little Japanese parsonage the day when the outgoing pastor asked her to tell him the best way to make a prayer-meeting profitable! What a brave young fellow he was! Disinherited for his religion, he did not flinch; and was loyal to Christian principles, even through his three years of military service! Her motherly interest led him to tell her how severely he was tested in the army. There were only a few staunch young Christians in his company, eleven all together, and the stronger were in the habit of watching the weak, and trying in every way to guard them from temptation.

One day he found a weaker brother surrounded by twenty young soldiers, all the worse for wine ; and sought to draw him away. At that they were angered, and surrounded him, determined to make him drink with them. When the young soldier came to this part of his story, he threw back his head and shoulders, and said, " I told them, ' There are twenty of you and you can kill me if you like ; but you can not make me drink wine.' "

When the new pastor came in, she went to the little parsonage again to attend his reception. What a funny little parsonage it was ! Built behind the church, up against a great rock, where a few vines only had to answer for a garden, it gave little space for the preacher's thoughts to wander when engaged in writing his sermon. A chair was produced for Aunt Mary; but the rest sat with their feet under them, on the *tatami*. The two rooms where the reception was held were such simple rooms ! No drapery, no *bric-a-brac*, no furniture even ! A few books and a graceful bouquet of flowers occupied the *tokonoma* (alcove usually found in a Japanese room); other than that, only the neatly made *tatami*, the thin, paper *shoji* (sliding doors for the admission of light), and the painted *fusuma*. Among the guests at this reception was a bright young preacher, distinguished as the first missionary to the Kurile Islands. He had voluntarily resigned his charge, and gone out alone to these cold islands of the North, where he received such a mere pittance from the Japanese Home Missionary Society that he was obliged to support himself largely by his own efforts. He was now going back rich in the unusual possession of a bride of his own choice. No scheming parents or fussy *nakadachi* (go between) had come between them and lifelong happiness. She was a Bible woman, well fitted, by four years of training and two of practice, for the new and trying life before her. It was a great pleasure to Aunt Mary to see this young couple started off from the mission-house, well laden with pictures and books to help them in their work. One of those with her, more accustomed to Japanese ways of thinking and doing, proposed to send the packages by a servant to the preacher's lodging-place; but Aunt Mary, with American spirit, responded, "Why, that isn't necessary! He can carry them himself." And the missionaries were pleased to see him, without hesitation, shoulder and bear away the packages, evidently esteeming manliness more than manners.

Aunt Mary was ever the busiest and happiest member of the household. Her ready humor, though directed quite unexpectedly at times in reproof of the tardy member or the willful one, caused the table conversation to sparkle with laughter, and every meal became a "feast of reason and a flow of soul." It was pleasing to note the effect on each jaded, worn missionary, who, in journeying north or south, called between steamers, and was persuaded to stop in the dining-room of this hospitable home. At first a light would come to his eyes at her motherly greeting; then a smile at some bright saying; at last, a hearty laugh, and he would go away cheered by the brightness and rested by the smiles and laughter, thanking God for sending this missionary to the missionaries.

Her conversation did not always provoke laughter; but tears came to every one's eyes, most of all to her own, as she told of an early struggle in discipline with one of her boys. He refused to obey; she insisted that he should. He continued to rebel; she remained firm. At last, unable to endure the pressure, he ran away from home. The father was inclined to yield, and begged her to forgive the erring boy and call him back. The mother, equally anxious, wept and prayed, and watched and waited for him to return, but refused to pardon him in his disobedience. When, in the course of the narrative, the wanderer did return, repenting of his obstinacy and willing to obey, smiles broke through the tears of all at the table, and a little of heaven's joy over "one sinner that repenteth" came into their hearts. "On his wedding-day," she added, "he came to me and said, 'I am so glad you made me mind;' and to-day he disciplines his boy just as I did mine."

The war-cloud continued to hang dark and heavy over the Korean horizon; and one of the questions, so long "laid on the table," was taken up and settled. Aunt Mary ought not to accompany the bishop to Korea, but, while waiting for an opportunity to go to China, could improve her

time by more journeyings in Japan. An invitation
to Hirosaki, pressed upon her attention since her
first landing in Yokohama, was now accepted. It
was not an easy matter to be the first to break the
pleasant circle in Hakodate; and Aunt Mary hesitated to name the day when she would be ready to
start off with one little missionary, in place of the
six with whom she had shared her walks, her letters,
her studies, and her calls, for one long, busy, happy
month.

The night first set proved to be stormy, and, of
course, it was not wise to cross the Straits in a
storm. The next night, after their tickets were
ordered, the wind seemed to rise again, and the
order was recalled. The following day the missionary unexpectedly succeeded in purchasing a
horse, which she had been coveting, and they must
wait another day to have that properly shipped.
But at last there came a night when they had no
excuse for delay. There was no moon, but the
sky was clear and the stars were shining; the sea
was calm; the horse was safely swinging in its
wooden hammock on board the steamer; their
trunks had been roped on the backs of coolies and
carried down to a hotel on the *hatoba* (wharf); the
house "boy" (in reality an old man) was strapping
their hand bags over his shoulders, and now, with
a lighted lantern in his hand, was ready to lead the
way. Good-byes were said to some, while others
accompanied them down the steep hills. They did
not talk much, for two angels of quietness were

brooding over them—the angel of farewell, and
the angel of the night. At this time, usually,
they were examining the mosquito curtains around
their beds, and preparing for a safe, restful night
in the home. But to-night they were to commit
themselves to a new and unsteady bed on the
great deep, and in the morning would awake on
the other shore.

They entered what was literally the *ground-
floor* of the hotel; identified their baggage, which
they found marked with paper tags indicating the
hotel to which they were recommended in Aomori;
paid for their tickets, and for the sampan which
was to carry them to the steamer; the hotel people had courteously placed two chairs in the sampan for their use; the "boy" stepped in with
them; their friends waved their good-byes from
the shore, and they were off—off in their queer
boat, whose oars seemed so strangely dislocated,
one of them propelling the boat from the stern. It
was very still; and, with the calm, such a soft, gentle darkness hovered over everything! The lights,
gleaming here and there from the shipping, seemed
to say: " We know it is time to be dark and quiet.
We are only shining for a little while to keep the
stars company." The lights of the city were more
numerous, and looked brighter against the black-
ness of the mountain looming above them; but
they, too, prophesied speedy extinction. It was
only the *Chishimamaru* that bore a day-time appearance of brightness and activity. With freight

all loaded, she had but to take on her passengers, and steam away at midnight.

The next morning early, she came to anchor in Aomori Bay, and was speedily surrounded by sampans, big and little. *Shioiya's* clerk, desiring to show special respect to the foreign guests, had engaged two boats—one for them, and the other for their baggage. They were not to be entertained at the hotel, they told him, but at " Suthon San no Uchi." He knew this well, as did every one in Aomori; for it was the home, church, and school of a missionary heroine, the one lone *seyojin* cheerfully braving a residence, winter and summer, in what all there knew must be uncongenial surroundings. They arrived before the telegram, which they had sent from the hotel in Hakodate the night before; so she was not expecting them. This delayed the breakfast, and made another delay in ordering jinrikishas; for Aunt Mary must escape, if possible, the usual hard *basha* ride of thirty miles over a road which, for two years, had been in the trying state of *being* macadamized. There was the horse to be intrusted to some one's leading, their baggage to be looked after, and a graduate of the mission-school in Hakodate, sent in their care to the Hirosaki school, must be started in the *basha*. After all these things were done, and another telegram ventured upon for Hirosaki, the jinrikishas were still nowhere in sight. Then the little missionary rushed madly about from one jinrikisha stand to another, until her calm hostess, who had

engaged them at the depot, where most of the jinrikishas had gone at that hour, found her on a corner, breathless and excited over her fruitless search.

This same hostess, with true Japanese courtesy,
had engaged a jinrikisha for herself, and accompanied them a good bit of the way over the smooth,
level stretch of road out from Aomori. Reluctantly
they received her *sayonaras* (good-byes), and proceeded on their quiet, solitary journey. Up to this
time the jinrikisha runners had endeavored to keep
abreast, but now they dropped back in line. There
were two men to each *kuruma* (jinrikisha). Over
good parts of the road, one was ahead to help, by
means of a rope, in pulling; but often he had to
go behind to push the wheels up a steep place, or
lift them over a ditch.

The tea-houses and little villages they passed
looked very different from anything Aunt Mary had
seen before. The roofs were thatched with rice-
straw, and the walls were made of a kind of thick-
ened mud or plaster. About noon the jinrikishas
halted before one of these mud-walled, thatched-
roofed tea-houses. At once a crowd of dirty, naked
children and a few men and women, as curious and
scarcely cleaner or more clothed than the children,
gathered around the new, white-haired *seyojin*.
The tea-house had no upper story, and only one
zashiki (parlor or guest-room). The crowd followed them into the yard, and stood gazing, as they
removed their shoes and entered the *zashika*. It
was very warm; but they must screen themselves

from this curious, gaping company. The *shoji* were torn and out of order; so *fusuma* had to be borrowed from the rest of the house before they were successful in making the sheltered corner they desired for themselves. Tea was brought, and with thankful hearts they ate the good lunch that had been put up for them at Hakodate. Then, leaving a small *chadai* on the tray in payment for the tea and their room, the little missionary called, " Kurumaya San, mo yo gozaimasu !" (Mr. Jin-rikishamen, we are all ready.) Once more they faced the unkempt crowd, and started on. During . the afternoon, growing weary of the long ride, Aunt Mary proposed a walk; and several times, in this way, they rested both themselves and the runners. It may have been in one of these walks that she quoted again to the little missionary a text which was often upon her mind during these days of strange experiences in Japan : " Partly whilst ye were made a gazing-stock, and partly whilst ye became companions of them that were so used." And then she was reminded of Amanda Smith: " Poor Amanda! She was gazed at because she was black! And how hard it was for her, until a friend, who found her in tears, repeated that verse, and told her she was following in the footsteps of the apostle Paul !"

They had now left the mountainous part of the road, and were entering the beautiful valley which contains the city of Hirosaki and outlying villages. All through the day they had caught

STREET IN HIROSAKI.
Showing "house with an upstairs."

glimpses now and then of the new railroad which was to connect Hirosaki with Aomori. It is seldom that the sight of iron rails gives the joy that these glimpses brought to the little missionary's heart. How many times she had been over this road in jolting *basha*, in bumping sleigh, on stumbling pack-horse! She knew all the ins and outs, the ups and downs, the stones, the hollows, the mud, the dust. Sometimes it had taken her two days, never less than one, to make this little distance of thirty miles. Once, night and a heavy shower overtook her long before she reached Aomori. She was denied even the poor comfort of a *basha* that time, and was riding in an open cart, which jolted her so that she did not feel sound and whole again for days. At midnight the cart drew up in front of a closed hotel. The clerks, the porters, the messenger-boys, all were sound asleep, and for a long time refused to be aroused. When, at last, they gave her shelter they kindly brought to her little paper-walled room the customary shovelful of bright coals for the *hibachi* (fire-box or brazier). Gratefully did she use these to dry her pillow and sheets, which, though serving in the cart as a cushion, were thoroughly soaked at the edges, and lay down to a sleep which even opening *amado* (doors inclosing the verandas, and opened at an early hour) did not greatly disturb.

Another time, after being thrown out in the mud, she rode into Aomori in face of one of the chilly, early snowstorms of winter, and was assigned by her courteous landlord to the largest, most open, airy *zashiki* in his house. He had thought to do her an honor, and looked surprised enough when she asked to be moved to a *smaller* room. He looked surprised again when, thinking to get warm *à la* Japanese, she asked that a curtain be put up at the unscreened doorway of the bathroom, and she be allowed to have her bath first and alone when it was made up fresh in the morning.

But the cold and fatigue of those journeys would soon be only a memory. It would not be long before the "iron horse" would carry her safely and comfortably, in an hour's time, over this weary way. Something else, however, was coming into view. Yes, they had received her telegram; and there they were, a great company, standing on Watoku bridge just outside the city, waiting to welcome them within. Hastily alighting from their jinrikishas, the better to return the low bows with which they were greeted, they walked part of the way through the long street with these Christian women and girls, their pastor among them like any true shepherd with his flock. They were passing between the same two rows of dingy, black houses which had often cast a shadow of depression over the little missionary's heart, and made her wish that Hirosaki was a little more like Tokyo, or even Sendai. But the shadow was lifted now, and no one in all Japan could be happier or more thankful. "It will be heaven enough," she thought, "to be met as we enter the other world by just such a com-

"AUNT MARY," THE "LITTLE MISSIONARY," AND HER WORKERS.

pany of the redeemed, who have washed and made
their robes white in the blood of the Lamb, because
we led them to the fountain."

But Aunt Mary had walked quite enough during
the day ; so she was persuaded to get in the jinrikisha again; and with more bows they sped quickly
down Watoku, out on Tera Machi—where the little
wood-colored church stood between a hotel and a
newly-painted, white photograph gallery, by the
castle grounds—and into Shiwowaki Machi, where
they stopped.   The high, black gate was open; two
servants with smiling faces stood waiting.   " Taiso
mate-orimashita " ("We have waited long for you"),
they said.   In the *genka*, Aunt Mary followed the
little missionary's example and exchanged shoes
for slippers.   They entered the box-like rooms.
Shoji and *fusuma* were all pushed back, and they
could look at once into the little garden at the rear.
Fresh nasturtiums, grown from American seed,
filled home and garden with their bright beauty and
wholesome odor.   "How sweet and fresh it is !"
Aunt Mary said, and speedily forgot, in the delights of this little Japanese home, that it had been
so hard to leave Hakodate.   She would have been
quite satisfied, after a hot supper in the little "six-
mat " dining-room (just big enough for six of the
mats known as *tatmai*), to rest quietly in her "ten-
mat " bedroom, opening at one end in a "four-
mat" dressing-room, and at the other on the garden;
but the little missionary would not have it so.   " I
want you to see my *up-stairs*," she urged; and, to

please her, Aunt Mary climbed the narrow, steep stairway, her low stature making it easy for her to escape a likely bump from the closet floor above. She was now in a true Japanese room (the rooms below had some glass *shoji* and two foreign doors). It had been an afterthought, having been built by an ambitious Japanese owner on the roof-top of the original house, which was a simple one-story house, like all the others in the street. So it had come to be known as the *naikai no uchi* (house with an up-stairs).

The *amado* were open, and with the *shoji* pushed back, a view could be obtained in every direction. In the shadowy north were the castle grounds of the old *daimyo*, whose stronghold was now only in the hearts of the people, who had ever been ready to serve him *shinu made* (unto death). "We must go there some day," said the little missionary. "It is lovely, the most restful place in Hirosaki."

All the missionaries who came to Hirosaki, loved the *O Shiro* (castle or stronghold). Closed, at that time to the general public, they were never followed there by a host of small boys, shouting after them, "Ame! Ame!" (abbreviation of America.) As soon as they had passed the other side of its queer old gateway, they were in a different world; away from the shouting rabble, away from the perplexities and trials, from the cares and responsibilities of their life and work in the interior. Every step in the broad, grand avenues of

THE "O SHIRO" AT HIROSAKI.

pines, every moment by the calm, still waters of
the moat, was fraught with restfulness. They
loved to linger on its ruined bridges, to gaze on its
strong towers, with only rusty bolts and hinges to
show the effects of time and disuse. The overgrown well, the neglected flower-garden, made
them curious to know more of former glories; so
they questioned the old people, who avoided the
O Shiro, literally passed not by it, because it spoke
to them too sadly of a past that would never come
again. One, and only one, description of the
daimyo's house was always ready. It was "*taiso
hiroi*" (very broad or large).

While these thoughts were passing through the
little missionary's mind, Aunt Mary had turned to
the east. The horizon was pinked with mountains, warm and soft in the afterglow of the day's
sunshine. To the south were more mountains
and more trees; terraced rows of stately crypt-
omerias, leading to the temple so often used for
sobetsukwai (farewell receptions) and the like. But
the crowning beauty was in the west! There a
second·Fuji rose from the waving rice-fields, to be
crowned, sometimes with clouds, but again with shining stars. The little missionary had often dropped
on her knees before the low window of her tiny
"two-mat" room, and thanked God for this mountain, which had ever lifted her up and away from
her surroundings. It could not possibly mean as
much to Aunt Mary as it did to her; and it could
not mean as much to her as it did to the thousands

of people who, born under its shadow, make their fasts, their offerings, their prayers, to the invisible god, dwelling, as they think, in the heart of Iwaki San (the usual name of the mountain, but also called Tsugaru Fuji).

IWAKI SAN.

CHAPTER VI.

AUNT MARY was scarcely allowed a night's rest
before the pastor called to ask her to preach for him
on the Sabbath; the Bible women called to ask her
to address their woman's meetings; and the school-
teachers came to invite her to a reception. Time
had to be systematized at once; only one meeting
a day; the morning devoted to study and prepara-
tion; an hour reserved in the afternoon for a nap,
and the evening given to reading and recreation.

Great preparations were made for the reception
at the *Jo Gakko* (girls' school). This building
was erected by native Christians; and as it had
never been painted, it was called, a little later,
by a new and youthful arrival in Hirosaki, the
"Natural Wood School." Only a limited number
of guests were invited to the reception; but they
were prominent as officers of the Church, or special patrons of the school. The girls were all
dressed in their best and brightest clothes, and,

107

with gayly-colored hairpins in their glossy heads,
looked not a little like an animated flower-bed.
The hairpins were not all surmounted with flowers; but some took on a new character from the
war, and represented Japanese soldiers standing
on headless bodies of Chinese and waving aloft
heads conspicuous for their long cues.

Speeches and songs of welcome were followed
by an address from Aunt Mary. She had noticed
their stooping shoulders and listless gait, so gave
the girls a talk on exercise, winding up with the
presentation of a bean-bag board. Her speech
was interpreted of course; but the little missionary
essayed to speak in Japanese. She got on very
well until she attempted to refer to a little incident fresh from the battle-field, which was just then
filling every Japanese heart with pride in his coun-
tryman's valor. A bugler, by the name of Shira-
kami Genjiro, though mortally wounded, refused
to give up his bugle; but, with his dying breath,
blew one last, clear, ringing "Susume!" (charge.)
His bugle was a *rappa*, but she called it a *kappa*
(meaning sea-monster, also rain-cloak). The Japanese audience, ever courteous and unflinching before even the gravest errors of *seyojin*, could not
endure this amusing change of words, but indulged at once in a hearty burst of laughter.
This quite disconcerted the little missionary, as
she had thought to produce far different emotions;
but she was soon set going again. A young man
in the audience, who was fresh from student life in

America, and so well knew the difficulties of speech in a foreign language, prompted her by saying, "I think *rappa* is the word you want, Miss ——."

The largest Christian home in the city was opened for a woman's meeting. It was the home of the popular representative from that district to the Lower House of Parliament. He was not a Christian, but his family were; and they, with all their relatives and friends on the street, were sufficient in themselves to make a fine woman's meeting. They had not as yet departed from country customs; but all who were married had a finer, more shining black polish on their teeth than ever boot-black put on a pair of boots. Though a well-to-do home, given to hospitality, it boasted the possession of not a single chair. The little missionary, anxious to make Aunt Mary comfortable, asked for *zabuton* (cushions), and quite disregarding ordinary Japanese proprieties, piled them on top of each other in the *tokonoma* (sacred alcove with a raised floor). There were old women, young women, and a few girls in the company. The younger ones had the advantage of birth in the same generation with a public-school system, and experienced no difficulty in finding the places in Bible and Hymnal. But the older ones, who, with a few exceptions, knew no *ji* (syllabic characters in which Japanese is written) until they became Christians and wanted to sing, were slow, and liked to sit where quicker eyes and fingers could come to their aid. Sometimes the younger women

would point with their fingers to the *ji* as they
sang; and the old gray heads, bent intently over
the page, would try to remember which was *ta*, and
which was *no*, and which was *shi*. When they
knew the words, they did not always get the tune;
but nobody cared about that, if only they were
"making melody in their hearts." There was one
obäasan (old woman), however, who was very
proud because she had once served in the *daimyo's*
household, and because she could read and write.
She always sang above and beyond every one else,
which made the young women titter and the old
women hang their heads in shame.

But all gave earnest heed when Aunt Mary began to speak. How they watched her face, noted
her gestures, waited for the interpretation of her
words! Her hair was snowy white, her years more
than theirs; yet how vigorous and strong she was!
How fearlessly she spoke—with what truth and
force! Physically, mentally, and spiritually, in
every way, there was the impress of strength—a
strength for which "sitting on chairs" alone could
not account.

One morning the little missionary was much excited. The young man, who had prompted her at the
reception, had come to request Aunt Mary to speak
at the *To-o-gijiku* (a large private boys' school, receiving aid in the way of English teaching from the
Methodist Episcopal Missionary Society, but not
friendly to Christianity).

"The teachers in our school have heard of your

fame, and ask you to speak to the students," he said.

Aunt Mary consented.

"The students do not like Christianity very well; so please be careful," he added.

"But I can not make a speech without any religion in it," was Aunt Mary's quick rejoinder.

"Yes, but please be careful how you say it," he urged.

When he had gone, the little missionary gave way to a burst of enthusiasm.

"Why, that is wonderful," she said to Aunt Mary. "Those boys are always throwing stones at our school. Once a stone came crashing through a window, and fell on my desk, when I was teaching a class; and since my first coming to Hirosaki I have not dared to pass near their buildings, for fear of being insulted in some way. This is a great victory. I am so glad!"

The morning of the speech dawned dark and rainy. "Shall we ask to have it postponed?" was Aunt Mary's question.

"O no!" was the little missionary's reply. "If they wish to postpone it, all right; but let us fulfill our part of the agreement, rain or shine!"

No word came from the school; so a little before the appointed hour they were shut into jinrikishas, whose rainy-day curtains were fastened so close to the hood that they were allowed only a peep-hole out, and rapidly drawn to the *To-o-gijiku.* Some of the teachers met them at the door, and

gravely led them through the hall and up the
stairs to a room thoroughly characteristic of every
Japanese school. The school may be lacking in
proper class and study rooms; it may be "narrow"
and cramped like the *Seiryu Jo Gakko* in Nagoya;
still it has its "teachers' room." At the *Hirosaki
Jo Gakko* one of the class-rooms was divided by a
partial partition, to make a place where the teachers could spend their off-hours, keep books and
papers, hold numerous consultations, receive guests,
and the like.

But the *To-o-gijiku* had a proper, entirely separate room for its faculty, and into this room Aunt
Mary and the little missionary were now ushered.
In the center of the room stood a table covered
with a white cloth, giving it the appearance of a
dining-room. They were seated in straight-backed
chairs near the table, while tea and cakes were
served in the usual leisurely manner. After partaking of these and "resting" for a full half-hour,
they were invited to go to the assembly-room below. On the way, the teacher, who had been in
America, was careful to warn the little missionary
not to walk beside him into the room, as that
would not look well in Japan, he said. The students—about three hundred—were gathered in the
gymnasium, and had evidently been waiting for
some time.

It was a strange coincidence that the subject of
promptness should have entered into Aunt Mary's
well-prepared address; but there it was—" He who

would be great, must be prompt. To keep thirty people waiting one minute each, is equivalent to keeping one person waiting half an hour." Was there a bright arithmetician among those students to compute that, at this ratio, to keep three hundred people waiting thirty minutes, was equal to keeping one person waiting six days? Probably not; and even if there had been, the sight of three hundred people kept waiting thirty minutes, or of one kept waiting six days, would have been alike, not at all startling or appalling to his mind. " Sukoshi mate" (wait a little) would ever come more easily to his lips than the crisp American " Be on time!" His "ima" (now or presently) was expansive, and might as easily mean to-morrow or next week. His clock—if he had one—would seldom indicate less than thirty minutes before or behind his neighbor's. But if the students, in the nature of things, were not impressed that promptness should be considered an element of greatness, they gave due attention to the grand old models of greatness which Aunt Mary drew forth from the Old Testament for their consideration; and the young man who had asked her to come could truthfully say, " You have done them good."

" There!" said the little missionary. " I am glad I have been in that school once; and I was n't stoned or hurt in any way, either."

The little missionary was anxious to give Aunt Mary a drive after her new horse. It was bought for a saddle-horse; but a horse was a horse, and the

possibility of its not being at home in thills did not
once occur to her.   There was only one carriage in
the city—an old phaeton, brought there by a missionary who had since moved to Tokyo.   A *betto*
(groom) was engaged to take care of the horse and
harness him to the carriage.   The first day he had
to wait outside the door for Aunt Mary to finish
her afternoon nap.   Suddenly there was a crash and
a shout.   The little missionary dared not move, for
she felt in her heart that the horse had run away
and smashed the carriage to pieces.   But it was not
so bad as that.   Another horse had run into him,
the *betto* said, and frightened him so that he had
started; but the carriage was not much damaged;
he would soon have it mended with a piece of rope.
He did mend it, but Aunt Mary refused to ride; so
the little missionary had to try it alone.   She
brought back such a good account, however, that
Aunt Mary consented to go that way to Fujisaki, a
village five miles distant, where they were to have
a woman's meeting.   The nap had to be taken first,
which made one delay.   The horse grew impatient,
so the *betto* went off with him, and was nowhere in
sight when Aunt Mary appeared.   Then, when he
did come, they had to go out of their way to take
in the young lady who was to serve as interpreter.
When at last they were fully started, it was time
for the meeting to begin.   Aunt Mary drove.   The
horse did not want to go.   There was no whip, so
the *betto* jumped off from his perch at the back,
and prodded him with a stick.   He went well as

long as the *betto* kept prodding him and running by his side. As soon as the *betto* returned to his seat, he resumed his former slow, slow walk. Aunt Mary slapped him with the lines, and made sad havoc with her voice in the vain effort to urge him forward. Again the *betto* had to jump down and prod him diligently with the stick, himself setting an example in running. Again the urging did not last. Over and over the poor *betto* had to be on his feet; and the patience of all was well-nigh exhausted when at last they arrived, very late, at the church, where a few women were still waiting for them. The meeting was to be held in a Japanese room above, used by the pastor as a study. Next door was a large public school. The pupils had just been dismissed, and were filling the yard and street with a tremendous racket. Pilgrims, too, were on their way to the mountain, adding to the noise and confusion.

It was difficult, indeed, for Aunt Mary to do more than talk to the interpreter, and let her try to make the women hear. They sat in a circle around the room, with heads bowed down in approved Japanese form. There were only two or three faces that were at all responsive. The others wore a dull, stolid expression that made it very easy for Aunt Mary to tell which of the women before her knew Christ and which ones knew him not. There were no silver crosses gleaming from their *yeri* (folds of cloth worn about the neck), no white ribbons looking soft and pure against their dark *kimono* (dresses); but royalty sat upon their foreheads, and purity and temperance shone from their faces. They were the wives of the leading men of Fujisaki, who, soon after becoming Christians, wanted a Church in their own village, had made it self-supporting, and filled it to overflowing with a flourishing Sunday-school. One of them had been a *saké* (native wine, made from rice) manufacturer, and habitually intoxicated with his own drinks until, through Christ, he learned a "way of escape."

As Aunt Mary and her company started homeward, after what they were obliged to make a brief meeting, they found themselves in a crowd of pilgrims. For many days these pilgrims had been busy preparing for this annual pilgrimage to the holy mountain. Their preparations had consisted in numerous ablutions and fastings, with purchases of needed supplies for their weary march. Dressed in simple cotton garments, with *waraji* (coarse straw sandals) on their feet, they were bearing aloft bamboo poles, each adorned with numerous long, narrow streamers, some of paper, but many of beautiful, thin wood-shavings, prepared especially for the purpose. As they marched, they sang, "*Saigi, saigi, doko saigi ii tsumi nano kai nano kin myocho rai*," which was interpreted to Aunt Mary as a song of repentance.

"A repentance that needs to be repented of," she tersely remarked.

The horse, like all of his generation, went much

better on his way home. It was not until they entered the city that, fearing probably he would be driven the longest way round, he suddenly made a sharp cut at a shop corner. Aunt Mary barely saved him from plunging into the shop and scattering the carriage and its occupants on the pavement. It was then that the resolution was quietly formed to use "Darkey" thereafter only for a saddle-horse.

Two or three days later they saw the pilgrims returning. The banners of paper and shavings—some for prayers, some for votive offerings—had all been planted on the top of *Iwaki San.* Their repentance was completed, and they were now rejoicing, with dancing feet and waving fans. They made a weird, fantastic picture, so attractive that all the schools of the city, even the *Jo Gakko,* had to be closed, and Aunt Mary and the little missionary were often drawn to the *roka* (veranda) by the fascination of the strange dance. Only a few women ventured upon the fatiguing pilgrimage, and they were glad enough to be jolted along, with their more exhausted brothers, in open carts.

"I am so sorry," said the good pastor of the Church to Aunt Mary, "that you should see our country's disgrace. This is my native town; but I have been away for years, and did not know it was still so bad."

"But I am glad," interposed the little missionary; "for now she sees, much better than we could ever tell her, the great need of Christian work."

No certain news or the war could yet be obtained. As the country did not seem greatly disturbed, missionaries thought it wise to open their schools as usual. Those who had been resting in Hakodate sent word to Aunt Mary to join them in Aomori, and, sped on her way by the gifts and parting bows of a grateful company, she started on the return journey. She had proposed to go this time in the *basha*.

"The road is not so very bad. I can just as well ride in the *basha* as not," she urged.

But the little missionary was quite determined to take her the most comfortable way; so two jinrikishas were ordered for them and one for the baggage. The man who was to take the baggage fastened the hat-trunk in his jinrikisha, and started off, refusing to carry more. This made it necessary for the multitudinous smaller pieces of baggage that had accumulated to be stowed on the seats with them, on their laps, about their feet, until Aunt Mary felt impelled to remark, "I think the *basha* would have been more comfortable than this." The little missionary did not like to confess that she thought so too, but tried instead to bear off the greater part of the packages. At Namioka, where they were to change jinrikishas, she hoped to make a little better arrangement.

Aunt Mary sang hymns along the way, and when they reached the poor, straggling village where they were to make the change and have luncheon, she said: "I have been thinking how

restful and free from anxiety I am, because I am
trusting everything on the journey to you! T'
is just the way we ought to feel toward our Heavenly Father."

The little missionary listened, but made no reply. Her feelings had been far from restful all the
morning, and she was still full of anxiety about the
rest of the journey. Crowded as they had been,
these jinrikishas must go back from here, and she
was not at all sure of engaging others in Namioka.
It would be humiliating to enter a *basha* after all,
and that for the worst part of the journey. Besides, the *bashas* were usually filled at Hirosaki.
While they were eating their luncheon she talked
with their landlord about the prospect. He was
very courteous; so she tried to be, meeting every
polite expression of his with one to correspond,
and working upon his sympathies for the American *obäasan* until he succeeded in making the arrangement she desired for the rest of the way.

Then she felt restful and free from anxiety,
quite ready to appreciate Aunt Mary's next words:
"I did not know, of course, what you were saying,
my dear; but your tones were very pleasant. I
never like to hear missionaries speak in a sharp,
vexed way to the Japanese."

If there had been time she might have confessed to Aunt Mary many weary struggles and
sore defeats on this greatest of all missionary bat-
tle-fields, whose victor is pronounced by the Master
himself as "better than he that taketh a city."

Like a child who tries to pump with the water
drawn off, and grows angry with the pump itself;
or another who can not find the beginning of a
tangled skein, and does nothing but increase the
tangle,—so she, not understanding the difficulties
before her, had often grown angry with innocent
results; not seeing the beginning of the snarl, had
increased harmless tangles, until she felt that, if
any one in Japan needed a missionary, it was the
little missionary herself.

At Aomori they met the missionaries from Hakodate, who had crossed the straits the night before. One looked haggard from seasickness; the
other had been ill all summer, and was not yet
fully recovered. She had with her a little Japanese girl, whom she had adopted when the child
was only a baby, thrown out by heartless parents to
make its own way in an unfriendly world. It was
a good work, Aunt Mary owned, but not the work
for a single missionary to undertake; so she had
said one day in Hakodate, " I would not let the
child call me mamma, if I were you."

"Would you bring her up without a mother?"
questioned the missionary.

That was hard, but Aunt Mary suggested:
"Anyway, I would not give her my name."

"What name would you give her, then? The
name of the man who disowned her?"

Aunt Mary was really cornered. Her judgment
could no longer hold out against her own mother-
liness, and she left the missionary in silence.

There was only one foreign bed in Aomori at the disposal of this party, and that was the bed of the resident missionary. This was given to Aunt Mary, and the others made themselves as comfortable as possible in a large *zashiki* at the hotel, their *futon* spread side by side under a great mosquito-curtain, which filled the room.

On the way to Sendai there was an unexpected stop. Floods had damaged the railroad, making it necessary for the passengers to walk some distance, while their baggage was laboriously transferred on men's shoulders.

There was a school in Sendai waiting to be shown Aunt Mary—a school for the poorest of the poor, who must be taught some simple industry, if the teaching would be effective. At the entrance of the school was a room containing a great bath-tub, for the confessed purpose of taking from the children the one thing they had in abundance.

There was a missionary, too, in Sendai, waiting to talk with Aunt Mary about starting a paper to be called the "Michi no Shiori" (Guide to Holiness.)

From Sendai to Yokohama, where they were to stay over Sunday! It was communion Sabbath at the Union Church, and, for the second time in Japan, Aunt Mary was offered fermented wine. But she let it pass untasted, for how could she remember the Savior's death in that which destroys those for whom he died?

A little rest again at Nagoya was made memorable by the passing of an imperial procession. The emperor was on his way to Hiroshima, the head-quarters of the army. Fully one hundred thousand people were in the streets; but for all there were so many, it would be difficult to imagine a quieter, more orderly crowd. Never a shout was raised as the imperial carriage passed. There was only devout obeisance; and after it had disappeared, a shower of fireworks.

At Kyoto she saw a large new temple, which was to cost a million dollars when finished. She had heard that the stones and beams of this temple were raised to their places by *solid* coils of hair, the precious offering of devoted women. A casual examination, however, revealed the truth. There was just enough hair partially to conceal the real rope beneath, so Aunt Mary said they ought to be called "fraud coils of hair." From this temple they went to another famous one, containing *only* 33,333 gods, one thousand being not less than five feet in height.

A restful Sabbath in Kōbe, followed the next morning by a climb up the mountain-side to see the waterfalls, for which their lodging-place was named the "Waterfall House." They were to leave the railroad now, and go the rest of the way to Naga-saki by steamer. It was not a voyage to be dreaded. For a day and part of a night, their ship glided over the wondrous inland sea of Japan. Fair as a lake, beautiful as a river, all who traversed her waters were sure to be charmed into sitting long hours on the deck, watching the ever-changing, often grotesque islands that dotted her surface.

There were a few hours of the open sea; then, past the rocks from which Christians were said to have been dashed to death in the years of fierce political persecution, they slowly steamed into the land-locked harbor of Nagasaki. Almost at once Aunt Mary's attention was directed above the tiled roofs of the long, irregular streets of the city, to a building set on a hill, where it could not be hid. She had heard of this building before. Its curious name, *Kwassui Jo Gakko,* had been interpreted to her as the "Fountain of Living Waters School for Girls;" and now she was to have the privilege of spending two weeks within its walls, helping to dispense the "living waters" in sermons, in evangelistic services, in personal conversations. How she rejoiced in the prospect, and more when she found some of the graduates of the school actively engaged in similar work! One, known as the temperance evangelist of Kwassui, had just persuaded a noted drunkard and gambler to forsake the foul and poisonus stream of intoxicating liquors for the living waters of health and temperance. About that time, news came to to the school of a young girl who, for the poverty of her parents, was to be sold to a life of shame, and made to drink of that vast river of immorality which is ever overflowing its banks in Japan, flooding and destroying all that is purest, best, and noblest. Never did a subscription-paper circulate more quickly than the one for this girl's redemption, and soon her name was added to the already long roll of the school.

In the midst of all the teaching and preaching, rose the busy sound of the hammer, for the foundations had been laid for a chapel and new dormitories. A hospital, also, was just opening, that the healing waters might be applied to the body as well as to the soul.

The family circle of Kwassui was enriched by the presence of several Korean missionaries, who had sought refuge, for a little time, from the dangers that threatened them in their war-invaded homes. With them was no less royal a personage than the younger brother of the king of Korea. He was consumed with ambition to follow in the footsteps of ambitious Japanese students, and cross to the American continent. With this in view, no one in the house escaped serving him now and then as teacher of the English language.

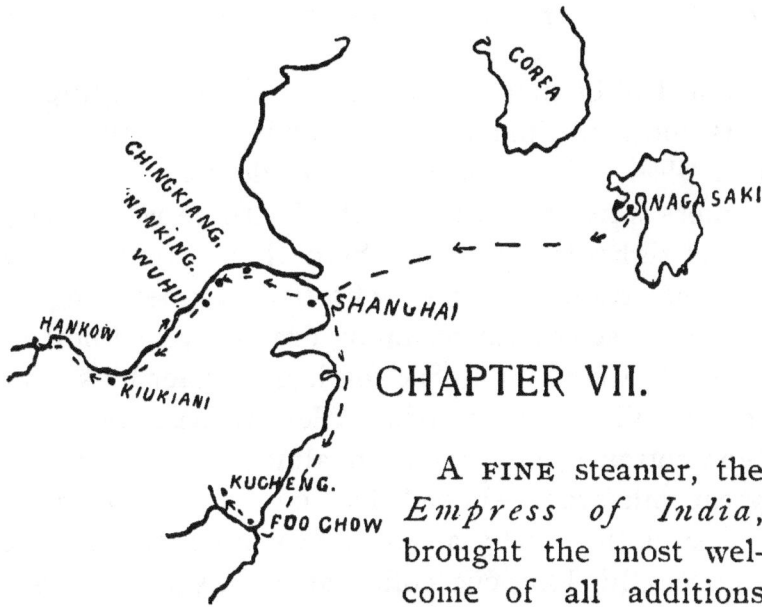

CHAPTER VII.

A FINE steamer, the *Empress of India*, brought the most welcome of all additions to the home at Nagasaki—a new missionary. But it also bore away Aunt Mary, who had spent five months in the East without yet "seeing Emma." She went in the care of other missionaries, who were on their way to China, and in their company the thirty-six hours' voyage to Woosung passed quickly and pleasantly.

At Woosung there should have been a railway train waiting to take them to Shanghai. The road was built—Aunt Mary remembered reading about it—but torn up as soon as angry Chinamen saw the great "iron horse" speeding over the graves of their ancestors. So, instead of rapid travel by rail, the passengers and all their luggage had to be transferred to tenders, which bore them slowly up the river to their destination. When they stopped, there was a busy scene. Most of the passengers

seemed to be making up for lost time by trying to
sort and land their luggage a little sooner than any
one else. These were old residents. The newcomers were content to wait; for there were many
novel sights to claim and hold their attention. It
seemed strange to those who had stopped long in
Japan, to see carriages again, drawn by real horses.
Even the familiar jinrikisha had a queer look; for
it was pulled, not by a trim little Japanese dressed in
blue cotton tights, his head almost concealed in a
great mushroom-shaped hat covered with faded
black cloth, but by a tall, lank Chinaman in loose
trousers, his long cue coiled about his head under
a diminutive straw hat. But a quainter carriage
than either of these was rolling by. They had
never before realized the possibilities contained in
the single-wheeled vehicle which they had known
from childhood as the wheelbarrow. But there it
was, with a partition in the middle making two
seats, just right for a man and his wife; or, if the
man was away at his work, the mother could still
take one side and have all the children on the
other; if a single passenger from the steamer
wanted to ride, his luggage made excellent ballast to
keep him from falling off. It seemed very funny;
but of course it was not; for the people who rode
never laughed, and the man who pushed them
seemed not at all inclined to amusement.

It was Sunday, and Aunt Mary was glad to be
carried, not in wheelbarrow or carriage, but in the
accustomed jinrikisha, to a good, quiet Sabbath

home. It was a boarding-house, designed especially for missionaries. The proprietor was a man
who had come to China to be a missionary himself;
but had concluded, after a while, that he had a mission to other missionaries, which he could best fulfill by providing for them this place of refuge.
And a refuge indeed it proved for those who were
compelled, over and over again, to flee from their
looted and ruined homes in the interior to the protection of their consulates in the Foreign Concession
of Shanghai. It was Aunt Mary's resting-place
while she waited for a delayed steamer to bring her
daughter to her from Foochow. It was not idle
resting, however. "She was preaching and talking and writing and working all the time," said a
lady in the Home, amazed at the industry of this
white-haired lady who had come to China to visit
her daughter.

Her work was interrupted one day by an invitation to dine at the Home connected with the hospital
and school of the Union Missionary Society. It
was the finest missionary residence Aunt Mary had
yet seen—built of brick, with spacious rooms, beau-
tifully-polished floors, and surrounded by extensive
grounds. It was gratifying to learn that this grandeur was not the result of missionary extravagance,
but that a wealthy lady had opportunely purchased
the house and grounds, as they were selling for
much less than their real value, and presented them
to the Society.

The hospital was an unusual illustration of self-support, netting one thousand dollars over the year's expenses. The reception-room was crowded with waiting patients, to whom a Bible-reader was dispensing the gospel. In the wards were women and children who, in addition to the pains of ordinary diseases, were suffering in their feet those other pains which a strange and cruel custom had fastened upon them forever. In the school near by were busy girls, with natural, unbound feet, engaged in spinning, weaving, and various industrial pursuits.

The same evening she was taken to see the various stages of a binding worse than that inflicted upon the feet. It was done by a little drug that, strange to say, had been pronounced harmless by a commission appointed in England to go to India to investigate its properties and effects.

Some of the binding-places were so large and beautiful that they were called "palaces;" others, so small, so filthy, and ever so filled with the smoke of the drug, that they were appropriately termed "dens." Into both "palaces" and "dens," young women, and even girls, were enticed, and made to share in a still more fearful bondage.

If Aunt Mary had been accustomed to restless slumber, she must have had very bad dreams that night. With all the evils she had seen and known in Japan, the women's feet had not been bound into tiny shoes, too small for a baby to wear, and there had been no opium-smoking; but as soon as its ports were opened to the world, the Japanese Government had prohibited entirely the importation of opium.

The next day there was still another trying excursion, which helped her to understand, as never before, how the Chinese world lives. Only a few blocks from the beautifully clean, broad streets of the Foreign Concession, with its rapidly-moving carriages, and busy, bustling, modern life, is the old, native walled city of Shanghai. Jinrikishas could carry Aunt Mary and her company only to the gates. Dismounting, they entered streets so narrow that, while examining the wares exposed for sale on one side, they might easily have fingered those on the other. They had to walk astride a stream of filth which coursed through the center of the street, and avoid as they could the piles of decaying garbage which stood everywhere. In an open space was a stagnant pond, covered by so thick and green a scum that some one facetiously called it a tea-garden. They were continually surrounded by crowds of filthy beggars, breathing out intolerable odors. It was not safe to give them money, for they would immediately clamor for more, and indulge in such pushing and pulling that it was difficult to escape without being torn to pieces.

At some seasons, other risks are involved in a visit to this native city; for it is in such places that cholera counts its victims by thousands, literally decimating the entire population.

At last came the day when word went through the Home, "The steamer from Foochow is in."

9

The mother's heart beat high with joy. It was seven years since she had given her daughter to China; and now on China's soil the precious gift was restored for a little time!

The daughter, accompanied by her husband and eldest son, had planned to join her mother in visiting the Central China Mission and attend its annual meeting, now convening at Kiukiang. All together they journeyed up the river. There was nothing to attract in the scenery; but as they neared Chinkiang, their first stopping-place, they noticed two gunboats peacefully moored in the vicinity of a fort. Upon inquiry, they learned that the boats had been ordered to Peking; but their commander, fearing to obey orders at such great risk, had decided to stay in a safe place.

The Mission Compound at Chinkiang, like many of those seen in Japan, was healthfully located on a hill. The air of cleanliness and good order pervading the buildings and grounds, presented a striking contrast to the dirt and confusion so recently seen in the native city of Shanghai. The sweet singing of the school-girls, and their prompt, earnest, and concise testimonies and prayers in an Epworth League meeting, were also refreshing and delightful.

From Chinkiang they continued up the Yangtse, accompanied by Bishop Ninde, who had his family with him and a large party of missionaries. Temples, pagodas, walled cities, now and then came in sight. One temple, erected on a mountain-top, sheltered devotees who were endeavoring to win the favor of gods by spending seven weary years in that lonely spot. At one place in the river a rock shot up two hundred feet above the water, so completely isolated as to bear the name of "Little Orphan."

It was evening when they reached Kiukiang. Sedan chairs were in waiting, and one by one, in narrow file, they rode through the dark, dirty streets of the city, the little feeling of desolation, which came in the darkness alone with the coolies, quickly dispelled by the friendly lights and cheery voices which welcomed them to the Mission Home. Among the first to greet them was the pioneer of the Woman's Foreign Missionary Society to Central China. During her twenty years of service she had worked in West China also, to be driven back to her earlier fields by riots, similar to those which, in later years, have so frequently devastated missionary domains in the interior.

The custom of foot-binding was so general in Kiukiang that it seemed wise for the new Woman's Conference, organized by Aunt Mary, to take some action upon the subject. They decided to call the Christian women together, and endeavor to pledge them against the custom. At the first meeting a woman whose feet had been bound for forty years, after listening for some time to the exhortation given, rose and said that she would take the pledge to unbind her feet. Her husband, who was in the room, immediately rose, also, to express his approval of his wife's action. He was glad that his wife was going to unbind her feet, he said. This was the beginning of several enthusiastic mass-meetings, characterized by pledges on the part of the wives, seconded and approved by the husbands.

At the close of Conference, before returning to Shanghai, Aunt Mary's party continued the journey up the river as far as Hankow, the head of ocean-steamer navigation. Here they saw the curious man-boats, pulled along by men on the shore, much as canal-boats are drawn by horses or mules. Sedan chairs were again in waiting at the landing, and they were carried through long, narrow streets, so densely crowded that they must have passed thousands of people; but try as she would, Aunt Mary could count but twenty-two women. She felt relieved to pass out of the crowd at last into the quiet and good order of a Mission Compound. This time they were entertained by English missionaries, who gave them an opportunity to see much interesting work. Besides a boys' school and hospitals for both men and women, there was a school for the blind. Here sightless eyes were bent, not always over books and papers, but often over baskets and mats, and the various articles in bamboo and straw which they were taught to make.

On the return down the river they had a Sabbath day's rest at Kiukiang. Before going back to their steamer the following day, they visited a large tea establishment, where six hundred men were em-

ployed in grinding tea and making it into tablets
for the Russian market.

At Wu Hu there was much excitement over the
war. The Japanese had been again victorious, the
emperor had fled, the viceroy was on his way to
Peking, the empress was dead; these and many
other reports, some true, some false, were being
busily circulated. All along the river they found
mission work seriously retarded by such rumors.

At Nanking, the ancient capital of China, they
made a trip to the Ming tombs, which are about five
miles out of the city. On the way they had abundant evidence of the spoiling through which the
city had passed during the Taiping rebellion, in the
crumbling gates and falling walls that they saw.
Their road took them through the Tartar city, whose
inhabitants are all fed from the emperor's table;
and as a result, perhaps of the good food, are larger
and finer-looking than other Chinese. Among
them, also, there are no small-footed women.

When they reached the tombs they found the
way to the entrance made substantial by a solid
stone walk, commanded by a succession of imposing gates, and guarded by rows of sentinels, also
in stone. These represented, not only men, but
lions, tigers, dogs, elephants, horses, and were without important members, one of them having lost
its head. The first gate was the most interesting.
It consisted of a slab of granite resting on the
back of an immense turtle, the whole carved out
of a single stone. It had stood there, some one

said, for five hundred years. They passed all the gates, walking to the spot where the emperors were buried. Here officials are required to come twice a year to worship and pay their respects to a dead royalty.

Near by they found the temple of Confucius, as bare, dirty, and neglected as any other. Besides the memorial tablets of Confucius, it contained some in memory of his father and mother.

There was another temple, filled with images which were intended to illustrate the pleasures of heaven and the tortures of hades. The gross, sensual character of the one set, and the cruel ingenuity displayed in the other, were a fresh demonstration to Aunt Mary of the ignorance and the horrors of heathenism.

What a pleasure to go from such scenes through a mission hospital and dispensary, then into a Christian school and home! The "stone cut out of the mountain without hands" was very small, but it was sure to destroy the gold and silver and iron and clay which man's ignorance and superstition had led him to worship; and though the great images, as they fell, might bury a few missionaries beneath them, their death would be like Samson's—a song of triumph.

At Shanghai, while waiting for a steamer to Foochow, Aunt Mary accepted an invitation to preach at the headquarters of the China Inland Mission. Here lives and works the founder of that unique mission, which has its forces concentrated

upon "only, and all of, China." An immense map
of China hangs on the wall of the chapel, and
man stands near with a long pointer, ready to ·
dicate the places to which reference may be made
in the meetings. Touching reports come in from
distant stations. One mission family is shut up in
a besieged city; another is about to flee on account
of riots; still another has been invaded by cholera,
and the death-angel has already borne away one of
its members. For all of these cases prayer, earnest
and loving, is offered; and messages, by telegram
when possible, are constant and sympathetic. Here,
also, new missionary arrivals are welcomed, and
given a "God-speed" as they go into the country to
the Home for preliminary training in methods and
language-study. The mission has a head; and so
plans for work, if not always the best, are uniform
and systematic.

It was late in November when finally Aunt
Mary and her friends embarked in a small coast-
steamer for Foochow. The steerage, which also
served as a baggage-room, was full of Chinese engaged in what was to them the most delightful of
all pastimes—smoking opium. With their huge
pipes, about the size and shape of a flute, in their
mouths, they were reclining in such a way as to
hold a tiny ball of opium at the point of a long
needle over the lighted lamp, which was a necessary adjunct of each man's opium outfit. The
ship was filled with this and many other disagree-
able odors. It rocked and pitched against a heavy

swell, until the whole party gave a sigh of relief
when, on the second day, Sharp Peak was sighted,
and they knew the voyage was nearly ended. Re-
embarking in a steam launch, they puffed their way
smoothly and easily up a charming river to the
landing-place at Foochow. Here, to their disappointment, there was no long row of sedan chairs
waiting to carry them through the narrow streets
and up the hill. They had arrived sooner than
they were expected; so there was no sign of the
grand reception that had been planned for them.
There was nothing to do but to keep the rest of
the party waiting while a resident missionary hurried on to order chairs sent back to them.

In a day or two, Conference opened with a communion service; and Aunt Mary had the privilege
of kneeling at the same altar with her daughter
and her daughter's husband and children, as well
as a large company of native Christians and missionaries. On Sunday she was happy again to be
one of a true Conference congregation. Even the
doors were full of standing people, and the bishop's
sermon went out to all with great power, in no
wise hindered by the effective interpretation rendered by the veteran missionary of the Conference.

At the opening of the Woman's Conference the
following day, an address of welcome was presented by a bright, intelligent Chinese member.
Naturally, it fell to Aunt Mary to respond. Her interpreter was a missionary's daughter, who had been
born and reared on Chinese soil, and was now a mis-

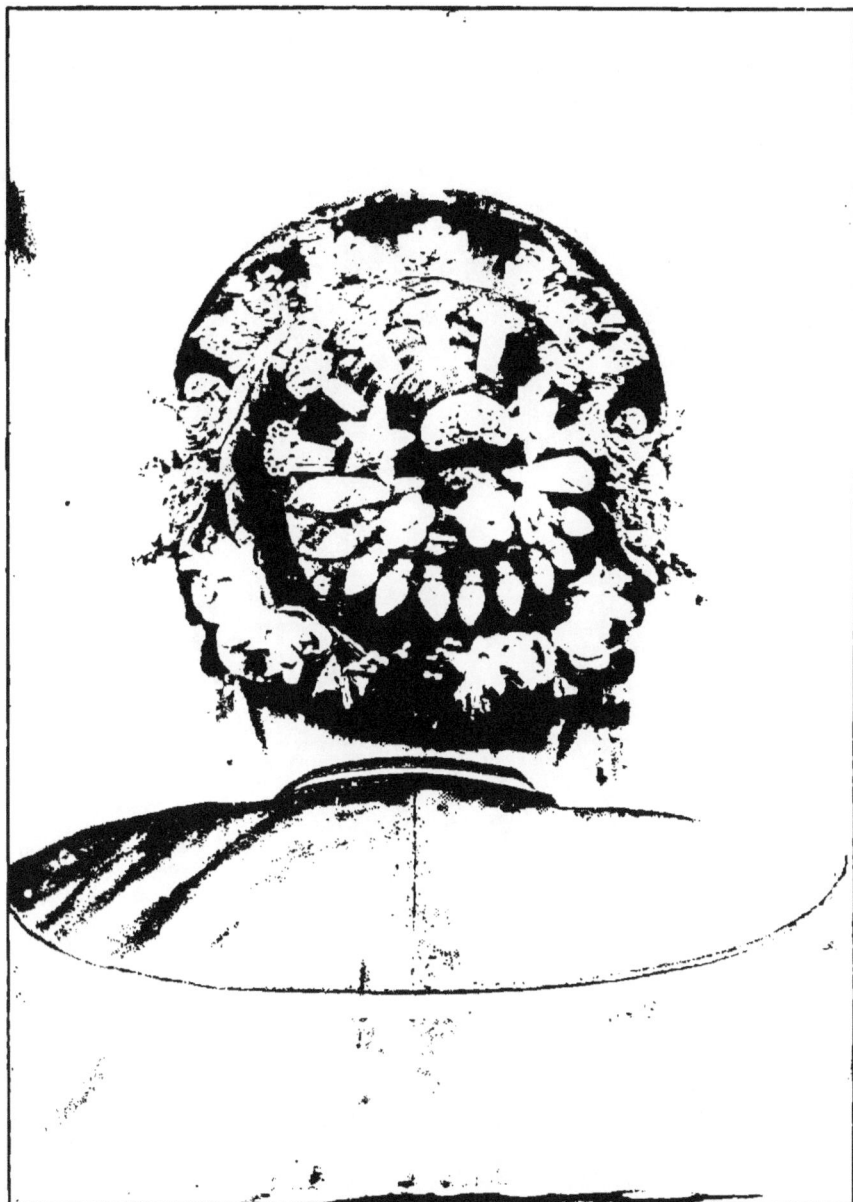

HAIR ORNAMENTS OF A CHINESE LADY.

sionary herself. Her interpretation was so ready
and spirited, that it was not long before Aunt
Mary began to speak of her as "my matchless interpreter." The native women bore an active part
in the discussions, which were all of a helpful,
practical nature, on such subjects as foot-binding,
intemperance, and Sabbath-breaking.

Wednesday, November 28th, was a memorable
day. It was the anniversary of the opening of the
Foochow Girl's Boarding-school thirty-five years
before. In the evening Aunt Mary addressed a
crowded house in Heavenly Rest Church, and
started a subscription fund for a new church-build-
ing in Foochow. The native Christians, with
their preachers and missionaries, proved to be
cheerful and even hilarious givers. Not a few
women drew great silver hoops from their ears,
and various ornaments from hair, neck, and wrists,
that they might have a share in the offerings. The
subscription amounted to fifteen hundred dollars,
preparing all the givers for a joyous thanksgiving.
Consul Hixson opened the doors of the American
consulate to the missionaries and their guests, giving them, by the aid of Chinese cooks, a true
American Thanksgiving dinner. The next day,
other Chinese cooks prepared for them an equally
elaborate feast; but, alas for the newly arrived visitors! it was to be eaten with chopsticks. The feast
was given by Mrs. Ahok, the widow of a Chinese
Christian of means, who began to give liberally to
mission work before ever he allowed himself to be

baptized in the Christian faith. The Methodist
Anglo-Chinese College of Foochow was founded
through his generosity in a gift of ten thousand
dollars, and was assisted by other Chinese friends
raised up through his influence.

There was much that was beautiful and attractive in this home—the silken hangings, the lac-
quered chests, the inlaid chairs, the lanterns, the
chandeliers with their wicks floating in open
vessels of oil—but the chief interest centered in
the young bride, who had recently been received
into the home. Her bound feet were incased in
embroidered slippers, which measured the highly
aristocratic length of two inches; her face was elab-
orately painted; her petite figure was attired in
handsome embroideries of silk and satin. She
did not appear at the feast, but was introduced to
the guests at a later hour in her own apartments.
Her wedding gifts made a fine display, a careful
distinction being made between the ones received
from Christian and those from non-Christian
friends. Among the latter were images of the
goddesses of mercy and maternity, which she had
already, no doubt, commenced to worship; for as
yet she knew not the "better way." What a
blessed thing it was for her that she had entered
a home which had received, before her, a more
loved and worthy member! To Him, though invisible, had been given the chief place, and soon
she, too, would delight herself with the others in
doing him honor.

At the close of Conference, its benefits were extended by erecting a large tent on the college grounds, and inviting the people, generally, to a series of gospel-meetings. They came; and in this Chinese tabernacle the presence of the Lord became manifest to others of his chosen ones, until there were one hundred and twenty-five people seeking baptism.

From this successful, after-conference gathering, Aunt Mary started on another journey, with the bishop and a few others, to Kucheng. A house-boat carried them up the Min River, and in its tiny sitting-room, which at night was converted into a bedroom, they passed three quiet, restful days. It rained during the last night, and in the morning, when they left the boat to continue their journey in chairs, it was still raining. After a little, however, the sun kissed away the clouds, bringing to view a succession of towering mountains, which, though varying in form and beauty, were all covered with verdure, being cultivated in artistically-arranged terraces. Sometimes their coolies bore them aloft on the heights, along the edges of steep precipices; but more often they were down in the deep valley, on a safe, level path by the river, which also varied,—sometimes only a shallow stream murmuring over its stony bed; then a mighty cataract, rushing and roaring over huge rocks and boulders. The scenery reminded some of the party of Switzerland. Later, a strike on the part of their coolies led them to talk of

America.   But every trace of similitude to other
countries vanished from their thoughts when they
entered the Chinese inn, which the striking of
their coolies compelled them to occupy for the
night.   In a cold, open, dirty court, surrounded by
a curious, ill-smelling crowd, most of whom were
smoking, they ate their supper.   When they had
finished, as one of the missionaries was improving
his opportunity to tell the "old story" to new
listeners, in came some Christian Chinese from
Kucheng.   They had walked the long distance of
fifteen miles to be the first to greet their guests.
How bright and happy they looked in contrast to
the hopeless, altogether-miserable audience which
they had unexpectedly joined!

The inn was full of fleas and mosquitoes, which
made sleep impossible; so at an early hour in the
morning their beds were taken up, and they continued their beautiful mountain journey.   While
still within a few miles of Kucheng they saw the
native pastor, clad in hired official robes, advanc-
ing to present his card and formal salutations.
Just outside the city gates others were standing—
preachers of the district, teachers of the girls'
schools, teachers and students of the boys' school,
and a great host of native Christians.   Of these,
the preachers and teachers only presented cards.
Fire-crackers were fired, making a noisy reception,
which ended in a feast of twenty courses, to be
eaten with chopsticks.   After this, our travelers
felt the need of the good rest which was given

them before the Sabbath work began. The Sunday congregation was good, though Aunt Mary was greatly tried when she saw the women, not merely sitting across the aisle from the men, as they had done in Japan, but surrounded by screens, that they might be out of sight. She felt better the next morning, however, when she visited the schools for women and girls, and thought of the sure emancipation that would result from their Christian training.

The sound of the noisy welcome to Kucheng had scarcely died away when the noise of farewell began. There were speeches, there were prayers, there were songs, there were presents; and again a great company went out to the gate of the city, all lingering over the parting as they had hastened with the greeting.

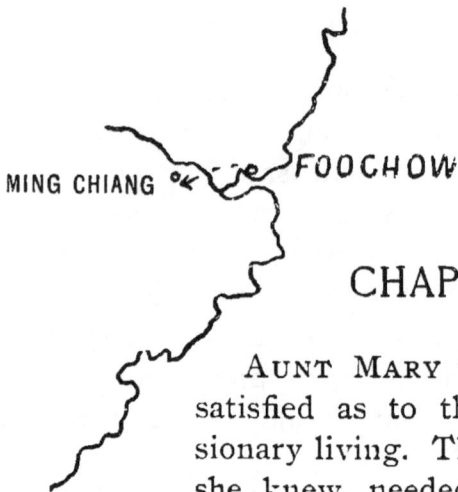

CHAPTER VIII.

AUNT MARY was not yet fully satisfied as to the luxury of missionary living. The Mission houses, she knew, needed to be large and airy on account of the summer's heat; but the rugs, the draperies, the *bric-a-brac*, the table appointments, often seemed finer than necessary; and the number of servants employed was still a wonder. She had once said to a group of missionaries in Japan: "Now, really, wouldn't you find it a little hard to go back to America and live again without servants?" To her surprise, one of the older members of the little group burst into tears. This missionary had once gone into her kitchen just in time to see her cook filling the tea-kettle with water still warm from the bath; and again, to see another cook moistening freshly-baked loaves of bread by squirting water over them from his tobacco-stained mouth. One of the brightest servants she had ever employed, presented frequent bills for broken chimneys, putting the money for them in his own pocket. The same "boy" made a duplicate key of the store-room, which enabled him to take successive relays from

144

the sugar-barrel to sell for his own profit. So, at thought of America's clean, honest, independent housekeeping, the wave of homesickness in her heart suddenly rose beyond control. But to Aunt Mary and other visitors there could not fail to come a sense of luxury at sight of apparently neat, well-trained servants, moving quietly about each mission home in the performance of their respective duties.

In her own daughter's home, she had now her best opportunity to understand these puzzling details. The house was quite as large and grand as any in which she had visited; but the family must include a single missionary, for whom no other home was provided; and the finest decorations, she learned, were due to the inventive genius of the occupants themselves. Then the carpets and curtains and pictures and ornaments, which furnished the house so attractively, why, the most of them she recognized as wedding-gifts! The table linen and the silver, too, had a familiar look. "How well Emma has kept her things, and how little new she has bought!" she said to herself, with motherly pride.

It was quite a company that gathered in the dining-room each morning, for many olive-plants had sprung up about her daughter's table. After they had finished eating, another company filed in—the cook, the house-boy, the washerman—so many servants, she hardly dared to count them. Then her daughter took up—it did not seem like the dear,.

10

familiar Bible—that book, full of strange, unintelligible hieroglyphs! But how well Emma understood them! Without the least apparent difficulty she read and explained a few verses to those who had just been ministering to her in other ways. Then they all knelt, while she presented their petitions, still in their own harsh, uncouth language, to the only Ear that can understand every tongue.

When they were risen, other books were produced; and though Aunt Mary could not tell the words, she knew the dear old tunes, and sang her part through in English.

Prayers over, the servants were dismissed and Emma went with her children to the school-room. This was the brightest room in the house, and wore quite an educational air, with its desks and blackboards. Soon the mother was facing her children—they were now teacher and pupils—and the work began. The school was divided into four grades, and there were only the morning hours in which to teach them; so a carefully-planned program must be strictly followed; no calls could be allowed to interrupt; all other work, all other pleasure, must be absolutely laid aside. In the four best hours of the day, from eight to twelve, she must endeavor to do for her children all that finely-equipped schools, with their large classes and well-trained teachers, might have done for them under other circumstances.

The dinner-hour brought a little relaxation to all. Then the mother put on her hat and went to

look after her other family. Thirty little orphaned
waifs, some of them found starving to death in the
streets, had at last a mother and a home at the orphanage. They came tripping through the halls to
meet her, and soon she was in another school-
room, teaching kindergarten plays and songs.
When she came out, they followed, shouting after
her the English "good-bye" she had taught them,
until she was no longer in sight. From the orphanage she went to the Anglo-Chinese College to
meet her classes there.

In the evening she went to her husband's office.
He was treasurer and business agent of the Mission; also superintendent of the publishing-house,
with forty Chinese workmen to superintend. She
found him poring over the proof-sheets of the " Re-
vised Chinese Dictionary;" and taking some of
them in her hand, she sat down and began the
fourth difficult task of her day. Her day! A teacher
in the morning; a kindergarten and college teacher
in the afternoon; and in the evening a student,
correcting that most difficult of all proof, which required, to do it properly, an exact knowledge of the
ins and outs, the twists and turns, of eight or ten
thousand different ideographs. It was not the day
of an ordinary wife and mother; it was not even
the day of her own busy mother in her younger
years. Such a wonderful succession of duties!—
never lessening, even on the Sabbath, only chang-
ing; for it would not do to give her children a
day-school and no Sunday-school. Then, there was

a vast number of children outside to be gathered in and taught of Jesus. Emma's Sunday-school numbered four hundred, drawn together by the magic of a simple picture-card, but putting to shame, by their attention, good order, and prompt answers, many another school in Christian lands, where the attendance is supposed to be the result of worthier motives. Aunt Mary was amazed; and instead of sighing because there were so many servants in her daughter's household, she would have been glad to see another, more competent than all the rest, to do the many little things the others never thought to do. Failing this, she knew no better way than to perform these duties herself, and went about the house picking up the washing, sorting papers and magazines, trying to relieve, if only by a little, the daily heavy pressure on her daughter's hands and heart and brain.

Christmas was drawing near, and invitations to various festivities were flying as fast as snowflakes in a colder clime. The first one Aunt Mary attended was at the hospital the day before Christmas. The same evening she went to the church to a Sunday-school entertainment. An elaborate program had been prepared, its participants ranging from orphanage babies to college seniors. The decorations were extremely showy—not only lanterns and flags and banners of all shapes and sizes, but lamps burning behind colored transparencies, and huge pink candles aglow with light and color.

On Christmas-day, the missionaries had a tree

A BRIDAL SEDAN CHAIR.

for their own families; and in the evening "peace and good-will" were manifested to the women and girls of the training-school.

The following day a special Christmas program was rendered by the older students of the girls' boarding-school. It contained one exercise, thoroughly amusing to both the pupils and their guests. This was the clever representation by one of the girls, in dress and voice and manners, of an American lady, another girl serving as her interpreter.

These entertainments were succeeded by Commencement exercises, until a welcome diversion was afforded by an invitation to a Chinese wedding. The bride was the granddaughter of the first baptized Christian woman in Foochow, and the groom was the son of the oldest preacher in the Conference. Two feasts were given; one by the bride before the wedding, to women only; and the other, at which the bride was not present, by the husband, after the wedding. She was carried to her new home in a closed sedan chair, used only for weddings. The top was adorned with a brass dragon; the glass windows were decorated with figures of men, women, and children; and the curtains of red, the bridal color, were covered with embroidery.

She was accompanied by a long procession of friends, carrying torches, lanterns, and the wedding umbrella of red silk. A band of music was aided, in its endeavor to make noise, by the useful firecracker; and if sound is its symbol, this part of the rejoicing was complete.

When the procession reached the bridegroom's home, the bridal chair, with the bride still in it, was carried into the court and rested on the pavement.   Here it was surrounded, not only by the invided guests, but also by many uninvited ones who had followed it from the street.   After a while the curtains were lifted, and the bride was borne away to meet the groom.   Their first conference must have been short; for soon they appeared together, her face veiled with strings of beads, his with downcast looks and solemn mien.   The ceremony was much like any other Christian wedding ceremony, only that the prayers and vows were in Chinese, and, to make it a more truly religious service, hymns had been selected for the beginning and close. "Guide me, O thou great Jehovah," was the opening hymn, and the service ended with "There is a fountain filled with blood."

Like most brides, soon after the ceremony she was compelled to retire to change her dress; for hers was a hired costume and must be returned, and her hair must at once be re-dressed in the style prescribed for a married woman.

January 26th ushered in the Chinese New-Year. Busy preparations had been made for this, the great day of all the year.   The women had been doing their annual house-cleaning; the men had been settling the old year's accounts, borrowing anew, if necessary, to pay the old debts; and now they were ready for their one day of rest.   It was kept as many another would keep a rest-day, the noise of firecrackers taking the place of the usual bustle of trade, and the making of feasts and giving of gifts filling every home with scenes of social revelry.

When this New-Year's was over, Aunt Mary accepted an urgent invitation from Dr. Sites to accompany him and his daughter, who was the "matchless interpreter," on a trip over the Ming Chiang District. The whole journey was a triumphal march, native Christians coming miles from their homes to meet them, waving branches of banana-trees (with strips of cloth attached to them for bananas), and shooting firecrackers for their hosannas.

Their best welcome, however, lay in the attention and loyal response given to their words of exhortation. At Lek Du, the meetings were held in the ancestral hall of a man who had been the Christians' most bitter persecutor. In those days they were not allowed to enter his home, and, if they dared to approach, were at once driven away with oaths and curses. Like another, he had boldly said, "What have I to do with thee?" but now, like that other, he was at home, telling all his friends what great things the Lord had done for him.

From place to place, from meeting to meeting! Sometimes their audience was a large and noisy one, composed mostly of non-Christians. It may have been respect for Aunt Mary's white hair, or it may have been some other gentle, sweet influence that subdued them; but after a little they were sure to give earnest attention to the new, strange

" Jesus doctrine," which many of them were hearing for the first time.

The meetings for Christians were even more inspiring. It was a coveted privilege to talk to some of China's hardly-redeemed millions—redeemed, many of them, from the depths of sin—gamblers, drunkards, opium-smokers, revilers, idolaters! How she would have shrunk from close association with them before their redemption!

Some of the meetings were for workers, and there was one mothers' meeting, attended by fully one hundred women. In a Chinese home where she was entertained, her hostess, who was still an idolater, promised Aunt Mary that she would now give up her idols and become a Christian. Soon after receiving this promise, an idol procession passed by. The idols were carried in sedan chairs. "*They must needs be borne, because they can not go.*" In the procession were bands of musicians, and men carrying banners, and, of course, the usual street crowd following.

The next Sunday Dr. Sites baptized many of the old-time followers in these processions; others he received into full membership in the Church. As he heard their testimonies, clear and satisfying, to the saving power of Christ, he could not forbear shouting with true Methodist fervor: " Hallelujah! This is very near heaven!"

It was nearer heaven for him than he thought. Taken severely ill that Sabbath night, he was removed to Foochow a few days later, and on the following Sunday the gates of the Eternal City opened, and he was shouting his hallelujahs with "the great multitude which no man can number," unto Him that sitteth on the throne, and unto the Lamb for ever and ever. With the exception of the daughter, who had been with him on this last trip, his family were all in America—too far away to come to his funeral, unable even to weep at his grave. Their absence made a double grief for the daughter, who, with yearning love and longing, turned for comfort to Aunt Mary, whom many of the missionaries in Foochow called " Mother Nind." " We, too, feel that our mother has come to see us," they had early said to the true daughter, who freely and lovingly shared her with them all.

The visits to the Anglo-Chinese College, where over two hundred students are in attendance, were always enjoyable. The college, largely self-support- ing, is exerting a widespread and powerful influence in the Fukien Province. Out from its halls young men have gone, not only educated, but redeemed, to fill positions of usefulness in the Government, in mercantile life, and in the Church of God. It was the joy of " Mother Nind " to have a Bible- class with some of these young men, who at the suggestion of their teacher, "the single missionary," were gathered once a week in her daughter's par- lor, and blessed seasons they were.

Politeness, cleanliness, and earnestness charac- terized them all, and made them very attractive to " Mother Nind," and she loved to talk of them as

her "dear boys." They, in turn, appreciated her
motherly interest in them, and on her birthday
presented her with two beautiful scrolls, which
adorn the parlor in her Detroit home, and often
inspire prayer for the donors and the college.

The consulates and Mission Compounds of Foochow are located outside the native walled city, on
sloping hills, that would be beautiful were it not
for the graves that make them like one vast cemetery. They are not the graves of missionaries
and other foreigners—for these are by themselves
in inclosed grounds, one English, one American—
but the graves of generation upon generation of
Chinese. "It is not true," a long-resident missionary said, "that they bury their dead above the
ground, simply covering them with a little earth.
They dig beneath the surface to a decent depth,
before they undertake to bury the body." This
explanation made them look a little better—those
numberless, nameless, grass-covered mounds, strewn
about in seemingly careless irregularity.

"When we buy a bit of land," it was another
who volunteered this information, "we must hunt
up all the men who own graves on that particular
plot, and make a separate bargain with each one.
If we can do this, the land with its graves is ours."
These ways, that seemed so strange and uncanny to
"Mother Nind" at first, soon became familiar; and
as she rode back and forth in her open chair, borne
by two coolies dressed in the neat blue and white
uniform which she had provided for them, her

MOTHER NIND IN HER SEDAN CHAIR.

thoughts were always of the living, seldom of the
dead. It was a trial to her to be dependent upon
any kind of a carriage; but Chinese customs did
not allow a woman to walk, subjecting her, in narrow, crowded streets, to rough, rude treatment, if
she ventured to assert her freedom. Safely carried
in her chair and accompanied by missionaries, sometimes of her own board, often of others, " Mother
Nind" visited many interesting places in and
about Foochow. Within the walled city, she entered one day a large court-yard, containing row
upon row of tiny cells, each about six feet high by
four feet wide. These cells are for voluntary prisoners, some of them offering large bribes for the
privilege of imprisonment. At times ten thousand
people are shut up here, making, with officials
and servants, a total population of fifteen thousand.
These prisoners are students who come to compete
for Government degrees. During the days of examination, each student is locked in his tiny cell,
obliged to eat and sleep, as well as work, in those
narrow confines until the examination is ended.
The successful competitors, who number scarcely
one out of a hundred, are conducted to a hall, as
plain and unpretentious as the cells they have been
occupying, to receive their degrees. The unsuc-
cessful try again ; and, if then they do not succeed,
still they try again.

Not far away was the "Bridge of Ten Thousand Ages," resting upon such solid blocks of
granite that it looked good for ages yet to come;

and the old palace, which had endured long after the royal heads that it once sheltered had perished with the Government that they represented.

Here, also, was another temple to Confucius, a comparatively new building, as the old one had been destroyed by fire. It contained tablets to Confucius, his twelve disciples, and many others, the first bearing this inscription, "Equal of Heaven and Earth." Only officials worship in this temple twice a year, with great display.

One day in early spring, the missionaries in Foochow were gathered together to celebrate a signal event. It was the birthday anniversary and farewell reception combined of a veteran American Board missionary. He was now seventy-five years old. Early in his nearly half a century of active service he and his wife together prepared the original Chinese dictionary, then undergoing revision at the Methodist Publishing-house. At such an age, after so long a period of service, their return to their native land seemed as fitting as the dropping of ripe fruit to the soil that nourished it.

Almost as interesting to "Mother Nind" was an invitation to supper at the home of a native preacher, the first convert won to Christianity by some of these earlier missionaries of the American Board. The respect shown to the wife and mother-in-law, the prompt obedience of the children, and the air of cleanliness and good order which pervaded the house, led her mentally to inscribe on its walls such titles as "A Model Family," "A

Christian Home," "A Work of Grace," "Fruits of Righteousness," and thoroughly to rejoice in the possibilities of even a Chinese household, when Christ comes in as a constant guest.

At Lu-loi, a village about seven miles from Foochow, she saw other wonders of grace. An old woman, who had from her girlhood been possessed of a spirit of divination, had been converted, and was preaching Christ to those whom she had before seduced. Like the " certain damsel" whom Paul met, she had brought her relatives much gain by her soothsaying; and they, greatly vexed, were persecuting her severely for turning from it.

Another, whose dissatisfied husband had taken unto himself two other wives, had found a true husband in the Lord, and was joyfully proclaiming his merits to others.

June 20th, the anniversary of the earthquake in Tokyo, found Mother Nind fleeing from an equally imminent danger. The sun had risen with scorching heat in the plains, warning the inhabitants not to remain lest they be consumed. Fortunately a mount of retreat was near. Only ten miles distant the beautiful mountain pass of Ku Liang rises to a height of twenty-five hundred feet above the sea. Here the members of the foreign community at Foochow have erected their summer cottages, or sanitariums. Many denominations are represented, but all have united in the erection of a little chapel, where they may refresh their weary spirits by religious services in their own tongue,

for which they have so little time during the year.
In this quiet haven of rest, on the first day of
August, suddenly a bombshell burst, which filled
the air with anxious forebodings, and darkened it
with the smoke of a terrible sorrow.   Two of the
English missionaries stationed at Kucheng had
been murdered in their summer home at Whasang.
The next morning the number reported to have
been killed was increased to five; and some hours
later the whole startling account was theirs.   Mr.
and Mrs. Stewart and six other missionaries had
been attacked early in the morning, some of them
in their beds, by a company of masked men,
and brutally massacred.   The five children of Mr.
and Mrs. Stewart, the youngest only an infant,
were in the yard with their nurse at the time.
When the ruffians had finished the work of mur-
dering the parents, they came out and attacked the
nurse.   Mildred, the oldest child, rushed forward
and bravely pleaded for her life.   "You have killed
our papa and mamma," she cried; "and if you kill
her, too, there will be no one left to take care of
us."   But, unheeding her cries or those of her
brothers and sisters, they did not leave until the
nurse was dead, two of the little ones mortally
wounded, and the brave Mildred herself lamed
for life.   In quiet Ku Liang, it was difficult to realize the full import of the tragedy.   The English
consul himself, thinking the reports exaggerated,
prepared to spend the Sabbath following in his
quiet mountain retreat as usual.   But he and others

in authority were fully aroused at last. Officials were sent to Kucheng to make investigations and, if possible, secure the murderers. British gunboats came to guard the harbor. A squad of Chinese soldiers was ordered up the mountain to protect the missionaries. Anxious days and sleepless nights slowly passed in their mournful procession. Why had God permitted it? was the thought in many a heart, and faith itself seemed stricken for a time.

But these Christian missionaries were not left long to grope in the dark. Light dawned about the promise, "There shall not a hair of your head perish;" and they began to realize *how* "the blood of martyrs" can be "the seed of the Church." Scarcely had the news of the massacre reached England when a call went out from the Church Missionary Society for ten new missionaries to take the place of each martyred one. This same spirit of supply arose, even in the hearts of the little children who had been so suddenly and cruelly orphaned by the massacre. Mildred was so badly injured that for weeks she lay at death's door in the hospital. When the nurse was bandaging the poor wounded knee one day, she said, by way of conversation, "Perhaps you will be doing just such work as this, here some day, dear." Quickly the child looked up, and with great earnestness replied: "O no! not here! I must go to Kucheng to take papa's and mamma's place." Some time, perhaps, we shall learn that the burial of the good is never a burial to decay, but to more enduring

life and growth in both this world and the next.
The missionaries will ever hold in grateful re-
membrance the faithful services of United States
Consul Hixson in the time of their danger and sorrow. Forgetful of himself and his comfort in that
heated term, though the martyrs were British subjects (the only American being our rescued Miss
Hartford), he at once planned for the safety and
comfort of those that were spared, and through his
tireless energy and undaunted courage, amid difficulties that can not be comprehended in home lands,
demanded investigation and retribution of the Chinese Government, and secured both. No wonder
that, on retiring from the office he had so nobly
filled, the Americans of the port of Foochow presented him with a picture of the Angel Monument,
erected in memory of the martyrs in the cemetery
of the English Church, framed in silver bamboo,
bearing the inscription:

PRESENTED

TO

COL. J. COURTNEY HIXSON,

U. S. CONSUL AT FOOCHOW, CHINA,

1893–1897,

BY THE AMERICANS OF THAT PORT,

In token of their appreciation of his official
services, and especially of his promptness in
sending aid to the survivors of the Whasang
Massacre, and his efficient endeavors to secure
the punishment of the perpetrators of that
crime.

The gratitude and prayers of the missionaries will follow him to his Southern home.

By the first of October it was safe for Mother Nind to return to the city, where cholera had been doing its deadly work all summer, laying low twenty thousand victims.

The wheel of life for her had nearly completed its seventieth revolution, and though it had recently whirled her through the excitement of earthquake, plague, and massacre, health and strength were well preserved. All her friends in Foochow prepared to rejoice with her as the wheel swung round to its starting-point. October 9th was the birthday anniversary; but the celebration, not confined to that day, began the evening of the 7th, with a beautiful gift from the employees of the publishing-house. It was a scroll of red silk, decorated with embroidered figures, representing Luck, Prosperity, Old Age, Longevity, and Cheerfulness. The next morning the givers came in to present their congratulations in person. Then the servants presented their scrolls. On one was inscribed these sentiments: "A woman can maintain her widowhood;" and, "The brilliant old star and the blossoming plant exhibit superexcellent felicity." Among other gifts was a spectacle-case, with the inscription on one side, "Let all the dust be brushed off, that everything may be clear;" and on the other, "You may obtain bright views of things by using these spectacles all round the world."

This day, beginning with callers and their gifts,

closed with a Chinese feast, given by the daughter in her mother's honor. On the birthday itself, missionaries, and members of the foreign community generally, presented congratulations and gifts, and an afternoon tea was served for them. The mails brought other greetings from over the seas, until the whole globe seemed belted with loving messages. Best of all was a liberal offering, presented in the name of the China and Japan representatives of the Woman's Foreign Missionary Society, in whose service so many of her birthdays had been spent, to assist Mother Nind in visiting their sisters in India. A similar gift was received from the Church Missionary Society missionaries in appreciation of what Mother Nind's abundant labors had been to them during the summer.

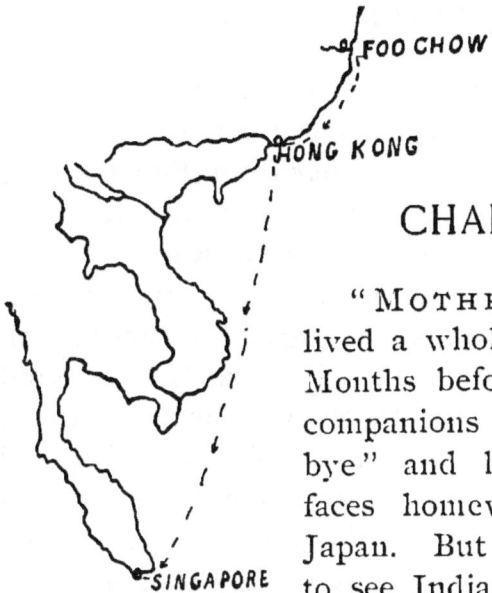

FOO CHOW

HONG KONG

SINGAPORE

CHAPTER IX.

"MOTHER NIND" had lived a whole year in China. Months before, her traveling companions had said "good-bye" and had turned their faces homeward by way of Japan. But she was longing to see India. Of all mission-fields, that was the first she loved, the first for which she worked, and the one she most desired to see. If only she could find a traveler who wanted to go that way! Her "matchless interpreter" was soon to have a furlough. Perhaps she would like to visit India! "Yes," she replied; but she expected to take a Chinese girl with her, and could not stop. Knowing no one else to ask, Mother Nind could only commit her way to the Lord, trusting in him that he would bring it to pass. Her faith was rewarded through a letter, received unexpectedly one day from Hirosaki, Japan. "I hear that you are going home by way of India, if you can find a traveling companion," the little missionary wrote. "Every one tells me that I ought to ask for a furlough at this coming Conference. If it is granted, would you object to me for a traveling companion?"

An answer went back at once, to meet the little missionary at Conference; and it was soon decided that they should start together from Foochow the last of October. And so it happened that the birthday feasts and gifts were also a farewell.

The morning of the little missionary's arrival the daughter was busy, as usual, in the school-room, the son-in-law in his office; so Mother Nind started out alone with the chairs. She was early, and had a long time to wait. As she walked up and down the landing, her thoughts were busy; not about the expected companion, or the country from which she came; not about India, the country to which she was going; but about China—great China, the country she was leaving. Her spirit, the spirit of eloquence that had moved her in other days, stirred within her as she thought; and with a few odd scraps of paper and a pencil she put into being her

FAREWELL TO CHINA.

China, farewell! Farewell to thy mountains, hills, and valleys; to thy rice-fields, and well-tilled farms; to thy rivers, rivulets, and rushing mountain streams; to thy bold and beautiful scenery; to thy trees, fruits, and flowers; to all the prospects that please in the realm of nature, where our Father has dealt with a lavish hand, farewell!

Farewell to thy narrow, noisy, filthy, crowded streets, where pestiferous odors, rising from accumulated heaps of offal and refuse, which lie undis-

turbed by road commissioner or health officer, are
breeding disease and death! Farewell to thy pov-
erty-stricken, depressed and oppressed masses; to
thy poor, weary toilers and burden-bearers; to thy
half-clad, half-fed millions; to thy beggars, blind,
lame, and leprous, loathsome and piteous to behold!
Farewell to thy dark, drear, and dirty homes, where
many generations exist, crowded and cursed by
heathenism! Farewell to thy ancestral halls, and
homes of wealth and plenty! Farewell to thy corrupt and weak government, for truth has fallen in
the streets, and equity can not enter! Farewell to
thy temples, shrines, pagodas, with their corrupt
priests, their multitudes of idols, their incense-
burning, and idol-worshiping; their pilgrims and
their pilgrimages; their gongs and bells that, like
the prophets of Baal, in vain call the gods to come
to the worshipers.

Farewell to thy myriads of graves, and the pros-
trate weepers and wailers, rending the air with
their hideous yells! Farewell to thy unburied, un-
coffined dead, waiting for time, or cash, or a lucky
day, to give them interment!

Farewell to thy degraded, dejected women, be-
trothed without their consent, servants and slaves
of men; and to thy neglected, despised widows!
To all the poor people who dwell in gross darkness, sitting in the region of the shadow of death,
farewell!

Farewell to all the happy homes, organized and
perpetuated by our holy Christianity; to their

family altars, and blessed harmony and love; to the
thousands washed and redeemed, cleansed and
purified, by the atonement; to all the native
Churches, with their preachers, teachers, members,
Bible-women, evangelists, and colporteurs; to the
noble band of missionaries; to the schools, Sunday, day, boarding, training, and kindergarten; to
the colleges and orphanages; to the churches and
chapels and homes, in city and country, where the
Word of God is preached and sung; to the tent-
meetings, Conferences, and Conventions; to the hospitals and dispensaries; to the blessed fellowship
with godly men and women, who have borne the
burden and heat of the day for love of Christ and
souls; to the graves of the martyrs and the cemetery where rests, in glorious hope, their sleeping
dust! Farewell! Farewell! To this land, rocked
by war, invaded by plague and cholera; on the
eve of a mighty revolution, which shall prepare
the way of the Lord and make his paths straight,
when the glory of the Lord shall be revealed, and
all flesh shall see it together! To the land where
rich harvests are about to be gathered as the result
of prayerful seed-sowing; where more laborers are
needed, and other heroes must come to take the
place of the crowned martyrs! To the land of
Sinim, of which the prophet Isaiah writes! To
this land, with its industrious, patient, plodding,
persevering, artistic, ancient, and in some respects
ambitious people; this cosmopolitan, yet conserva-
tive race, with its ancient literature, its classics !

To this land, where the New Testament is now in the hands of the emperor and empress; this land, for which more prayers are offered, and toward which more eyes are turned, than ever before! Land of contrasts; of ignorance and knowledge; of poverty and wealth; of darkness and light; of idolatry and Christianity; land of science, and land of slavery; a land of immense undeveloped resources, where millions yet lack the necessities of life! Land of Confucius, and land of Sinim, farewell! Still we love thee and laud thee, and pity and pray for thee, believe and expect great things of thee; for China shall be a redeemed people! China, our China! Farewell! farewell!

Her passage was engaged in the good ship *Formosa,* a cargo steamer of the P. and O. line. Besides the little missionary, she would have the company, as far as Singapore, of the "matchless interpreter," with her Chinese protégés, the three surviving children of the Stewart family, their aunt who had come from England for them, and a lady missionary of the Church of England, who was broken down in health and must return home.

The parting with her grandchildren, though she expected to see them the following year in America, was harder even than saying farewell to China. After the good-bye kisses had all been given, the one little girl, Alice, put up her hands again, saying, "I want to love you more, grandma." There were others who wanted to "love her more." The

single missionary, whose room had been next to
hers, thought how she would miss the " morning
meeting," as she called it, when Mother Nind sang
hymns over her bath.   Many of the missionaries
accompanied her to the steamer, and knelt about
her in her tiny cabin to hear themselves prayed for
again.   She had entered so into the details of their
life that she had seemed like one of them.   Many
a little reform on the Mission Compound had been
due to her energy and perseverance.   Among the
things that had grieved her was the delivery of
mail on the Sabbath.   The missionaries had not
thought it possible to do other than receive it; but
through her enterprise, a petition, which was
granted, was sent to the post-office authorities requesting the retention of all mission mail that
might come on Sunday, until Monday.

   Others besides Mother Nind's friends were at
the steamer.   One, a tall English missionary, was
so completely disguised in his shaven head, long
cue, and Chinese dress, that the little missionary
mistook him for a real Chinaman.

   " Do you think it is better for the missionaries
to wear the native dress?" she asked Mother Nind.

   " I do n't know " was the reply.   " It certainly
does not save them from being massacred; for all
who were killed at Whasang wore the Chinese
dress."

   " I wonder if they are as particular as the Japanese about the various details of their costume?"
commented the little missionary.

"They notice every fold and knot so closely that if a missionary wants to escape criticism, she is better off in her own dress. Just before leaving Japan I heard one of our preachers severely criticise the Salvation Army officers, who have recently arrived, dressed in Japanese clothes, made in England. He said: 'They call themselves an army; but our soldiers do not go to the battle-field in loose, flowing sleeves and skirts. They have adopted the close, military dress, approved by other natives. Then they are preachers; but what one of our preachers has not a foreign dress to wear, when he enters his pulpit?'"

As in most English steamers, the officers of the *Formosa* sat at the same table with the passengers. With the exception of the captain, who was opposed to argument, they seemed determined to throw down some challenge for debate at every meal. At such times the missionaries were glad, indeed, to have a champion like Mother Nind on their side. One day the subject was temperance. An officer remarked, "The Bible is opposed to total abstinence." She replied only by quoting such passages as "Wine is a mocker, strong drink is raging," and "Look not upon the wine when it is red," etc., with special emphasis on the work "*look.*" That officer subsided, and another took up the strain: "But I *fancy* [pronounced fähncy] that the wine the Savior made was the strongest of intoxicating beverages." "Fancy has no place in an argument," quickly replied Mother

Nind, and that debate was ended. Again, when Moody and other prominent evangelists were assailed, she listened for a while, then quietly remarked: "Excuse me, gentlemen, but I am personally acquainted with those workers; and am happy to inform you that the things you say of them are not true."

Another time she heard some one flippantly remark, "All's well that ends well." And, quick as a flash, replied, "Yes, but I want *well* to begin on."

But, debating as they so often did on the wrong side, they were ever kind and courteous, vying with each other in gentleness and tender attention to the wants of the lame Mildred, who had to be carried on deck each day. Kathleen, the next younger, in her rosy cheeks and active play, presented a striking contrast to the pale, quiet sister. She was quite as mature, however, in her care of the little brother, never allowing him to make any moves that seemed at all dangerous.

Evan, the youngest, was still troubled by bad dreams, in which he saw the dreadful Chinamen coming again to take him; and often he awoke in the night screaming with terror. But one morning, as his aunt was preparing his breakfast, he looked up with a bright smiling face and said, "God was very good to me last night, and gave me no bad dreams." He was a very thoughtful little fellow; so when she asked him, "Evan, do you think I love you?" he replied with another question: "Why did you come so far to get me?"

The *Formosa* made her first stop at Hong Kong, and Mother Nind improved the opportunity to tread once more on safe and solid English soil. Many times she remarked, " How good it is to be on a bit of land under the protection of the English Government!"

The captain had said, " There are two nice trips to make in Hong Kong, one to ' Happy Valley,' and the other to the ' Peak.' " So, after wandering about in the shops a little, she and her companions engaged jinrikishas to take them to "Happy Valley." It was only a short ride from the city to the beautiful dale which bore the name of " Happy Valley," and which they found contained a race-course and a graveyard,—pleasure for the living and rest for the dead. The cemetery was extensive, containing separate divisions for Jew and Mohammedan, Protestant and Catholic. The Protestant was most attractive, with its flower-beds and fountains, its palms and other tropical trees, which were growing in great luxuriance. It would have seemed like a park had it not been for numerous white stones, telling their sad tale of death and decay, and for many newly-made graves yawning to receive the dead that incoming ships were sure to bring.

From " Happy Valley " their jinrikisha runners (Chinese) drew them rapidly to the tram-station on the hill. Every one said it was perfectly safe— that cable-line up the mountain, which looked almost as near a perpendicular as an elevator! So they ventured to undertake the trip. Noticing 1, 2, and 3 in big figures, on the various compartments of the car, Mother Nind said, "Now I'll save my money, and go third-class." Her companions followed her example, passing by the luxurious, inclosed, first-class compartment, to take as good places as they could find in the open seats outside. Pretty soon the car started. How very steep it was! It made them dizzy to look up or down or sideways. All at once the car stopped still on that dreadful perpendicular. Hearts bounded to mouths, where they staid until it went on again. After a little the incline became more gradual; then another steep place, and again the car stopped. "I believe they stop just to show how well they can hold the car!" the little missionary indignantly exclaimed. But the conductor was collecting fares.

"Fifty cents, please," he said.

"But we are riding third-class," Mother Nind replied.

"Pardon me, madam, but you are in a seat reserved for first-class smokers."

The train did not take them to the top, but left them near the Peak House, where they had planned to have luncheon. Here another surprise awaited them, for the Peak House was not a mountain booth, where they could buy cold boiled eggs and sandwiches, but a fine hotel, with lovely grounds, and no meals less than seventy-five cents.

"It seems impossible to make this a cheap trip. I'm afraid I shall have to spend my Foochow souvenirs," said Mother Nind; and she took them out of her purse as she spoke. They were two Mexican dollars; one clean and smooth as it had come from the mint; the other showing much use, and so indented in the middle that it would hold water. "The Chinese in Foochow hammer every coin before they accept it, to make sure that it is genuine," she explained to the little missionary.

"That is better than the way they do in West China. It must be very inconvenient to have only strings of copper cash and silver bullion, which must be weighed as it is used. But those will be very curious at home, and you must n't spend them. I will settle this bill, and you can pay me when you get the first installment on your letter of credit," said the little missionary.

The remainder of the distance to the Peak had to be made by actual climbing; and though the path led over a broad, beautiful concrete walk, with many delightful resting-places along the way, they were all tired enough when they reached the Peak itself. But there was plenty to rest them in the view from the highest point of the lovely mountainous island of Hong Kong. There was the broad, blue sea; the quiet harbor, full of shipping, their own big steamer looking as tiny as any at that height; the strong, substantial buildings of this English town in the "far East;" the beautiful homes on the mountain!

"How high is this mountain?" asked Mother Nind of the signal-station man.

"Eighteen hundred and twenty-five feet," he replied.

"Just the year in which I was born," she remarked; and the others thought that, with the aid of that mnemonic, they, too, might remember.

Their fifty cents fare up the mountain had included a return ticket, so they went down in style in the luxurious first-class compartment. On the way, the " matchless interpreter " said:

"I wonder if we can't get some soda-water here. I feel very thirsty."

"So do I, and especially for soda-water," chimed in the little missionary; "for I have n't had any since I went to Japan, over five years ago."

People are never so foolish on land as when they have been at sea a little while; so they dragged their weary limbs about the streets of Hong Kong, hunting for soda-water, until they were fully convinced there was none.

"Is n't it strange that the English do n't care for soda-water?" said these tired, thirsty Americans, as they finished their day by buying bottled lemonade on the steamer.

"How did you like ' Happy Valley?' " and " Did you climb to the ' Peak?' " were the inquiries that came from the ship's officers.

"That train is fearful, is n't it?" said the stewardess. "When I got off, I just said, 'Thank God!' and I never wanted to go on again."

That evening, as the little missionary was engaged in conversation with the captain about the differences in the English language, as spoken by the English and the Americans, she said:

"I learned a new word last night."

"What is that?" asked the captain.

"In America, when we wish to speak of the number of guests to be served at a dinner, we say, 'There are so many plates, or so many covers;' but you say ' forms.'"

The captain looked puzzled.

"Last night, when I asked the stewardess if we could have an early breakfast, as we wanted to go ashore, she asked me, 'How many forms?'"

Still the captain looked puzzled, and said that he had never heard that word before.

The little missionary was disconcerted; but thought that she would speak to Mother Nind about it, as she was English born and bred. Mother Nind did not know the word, so she went to the stewardess herself to ask her what she said.

"I said, 'How many for, Miss?'" the stewardess replied.

Soon after leaving Hong Kong, the *Formosa* was attacked by a monsoon, and for two or three days was rocked as violently as a cradle by a small boy who is in a hurry to get the baby to sleep, and be off to a game of ball. Early in the storm the little missionary was thrown on the floor. Then the side-pieces were all put in, and the berths made secure; the steamer chairs were lashed to the deck; a full set of racks was placed on the table, and the passengers learned to be dextrous in balancing plates of soup and cups of coffee in their hands; for the entire contents would spill, if allowed to rest on the table. Sometimes they did not feel like taking soup or coffee, but were content to lie in their berths, or on the cushioned seats of the saloon, listening to the swish-swash of the water as it came into the lower deck. Occasionally the monotony was relieved by a crash and the sound of voices:

"How many smashed?"

"Only one!" came the cheery answer.

Mother Nind was a good sailor, and continued her walks on deck, though she could take few steps without the aid of an officer's arm. To see her trying to walk on a floor that was constantly playing see-saw, now up, now down, one could readily believe what the captain of an Atlantic steamer once said of her: "There's a passenger who has walked half way across the ocean."

By the 12th of November the sea was calm again. Writing materials were brought out once more, and letters prepared to mail at Singapore. As the little missionary was writing the date, suddenly she exclaimed, "Why, this is my birthday!" The "matchless interpreter" heard the words, and passed them on. The next evening, at dinner, a fine birthday cake ornamented the table, and the little missionary unexpectedly found herself the recipient of the congratulations of all on board.

As they neared Singapore, Mother Nind's heart

overflowed with joy. "I could not sleep last night," she said to the little missionary; "but lay awake much of the time, praising the Lord for bringing me to Singapore." Then she told the story of how the Woman's Foreign Missionary Society opened work in Singapore: "Bishop Harris had just returned from a trip around the world, and reported it to be the wickedest place he had ever seen, with street after street containing not one decent house of any kind. Our general executive meeting, at Evanston, Illinois, appointed a committee to consider the advisability of opening work there. Their report was short and unfavorable. There was too little money in the treasury to undertake work in such a new and difficult field, they said. As the report was about to be accepted, I felt impelled to rise and move that the committee be requested to frame a new report favorable to the work; that I would take, not merely a *dip*, but a *plunge* of faith, and pledge the Minneapolis Branch for three thousand dollars. My motion prevailed, and I had to go to work to raise the money. When I had fifteen hundred dollars, I began to pray for a worker. Strange to say, as I prayed in America, God answered my prayer in Australia. It was when Miss Leonard was there, conducting evangelistic services. Through her efforts, Miss Sophia Blackmore was led to consecrate herself to foreign missionary work, and. after a few months in India, accepted our appointment to Singapore. She has been here nine years; and,

though I have been corresponding with her all
that time, I shall see her for the first to-day."

It had been raining, and the decks were quite
wet when Mother Nind and her companion ventured out for a good look at their equatorial surroundings. "It's always raining in Singapore,"
one of the officers said. Just ahead was a beautiful group of palms, spreading their leaves in the
form of huge fans; and a village of huts, built on
piles over the water; on the roadway leading to the
pier, open carts were approaching, drawn by fat,
sleepy-looking, white bullocks; and nearing the
ship by water was a boat, loaded with great red
and white corals.

"When you land," the captain said, "you must
take a *gari* for yourselves, and a bullock cart for
your luggage;" and he kindly deputed one of his
officers to help them ashore and engage the proper
vehicles for them. Half wondering what a *gari*
could be, they hastily gathered their luggage together, said good-bye to the passengers they were
to leave behind, and hastened ashore. The *gari*
proved to be neither jinrikisha nor sedan chair, but
a closed carriage, with two seats inside for passengers, and a driver's seat outside. One poor little
pony had to supply the motive power; but it
moved rapidly, every step causing the *gari* to rat-
tle so that the occupants had to shout to make
each other hear. Their road lay first over a bit of
the country lying low and wet from recent rains.
Then streets came into view, a disused street-car

MARY C. NIND DEACONESS HOME.

road, and trees and foliage, new and many of them
unknown to our travelers. The driver seemed uncertain how to find the address which they had given
him, so they were relieved when they discovered
the sign, "Sophia Road," and knew that they were
going in the right direction. "I have a great many
S's to make, when I direct a letter to Miss Blackmore," Mother Nind said. "It's Miss Sophia
Blackmore, Sophia Road, Singapore, Straits Settlements."

But, already they had entered the grounds of
the "Mary C. Nind Deaconess Home," and Miss
Blackmore was coming down the steps to meet
them. The ground-floor was occupied by the
children of the Home, while the deaconesses
lived above; so they were invited to ascend the
stairs, which were on the outside, leading to the
upper veranda. The veranda was broad, and furnished with chairs and tables like a sitting-room.
It opened into the drawing-room, where our party
were attracted, first of all, to a large portrait of
Mother Nind, which seemed to be there to welcome them to her own home. But after removing
hats and wraps, they preferred to sit in the veranda.

"What is this great tree in front, covered with
large, drooping leaves?" some one asked.

"We call that the 'umbrella-tree,'" was the
reply.

"And what is that yonder, covered with bright,
scarlet blossoms?"

" That's the ' flaming forest.' "

What wonderful trees, what palms, what ferns, what spreading luxuriance, and in the middle of November, high time for snow to be flying in other lands!

These reflections were interrupted by a step on the stairs. What a weary step it was! When the face appeared, it was thin and pallid to correspond. She was another of Mother Nind's missionary daughters, who had been out less than three years, but was already "breaking down." She confessed that she was overworking, and promised to try to give up some of her work. Then Miss Blackmore was called down-stairs. The bullock-cart had come with the baggage. When she returned she said:

" The man wanted more money than you told me to pay."

" Did you give it to him?"

"Yes. I thought it wiser not to have any trouble with him."

There he was, driving off with his cart—a cloth wound around his head for a turban, another about his loins; and, for the rest, a dark, shining skin his only covering. It *was* wiser not to have any trouble with *him.*

"My head aches, and I feel badly. Will you give me a place to lie down?" asked the little missionary.

After awhile the "matchless interpreter" came in.

THE BULLOCK CART.

"My head aches dreadfully," she said, "and I can hardly breathe. I feel as if I were shut up in a hot-house, the air is so close and steamy."

"That must be what's the matter with me," said the little missionary. "It's the air. I wondered what could give me such a headache."

After lunching on honey, bread and butter, and delicate, fresh plantains, they felt better, and were ready to go to the steamer; for the "matchless interpreter" and her companion, sweet Margaret Wong, must continue their journey on the *Formosa*. The new mission *gari* was ordered for them. On the way it began to rain. The nice, fresh curtains were taken out, and they were shut in as quickly as possible.

"This rain is full of malaria," the accompanying missionary said. "We have to be very careful not to get the least drop on us."

A little later the "matchless interpreter" called out to the little missionary, "There's a drop of malaria on you," and mischievously hastened to brush it off.

They had arrived at the landing, where they expected to find a boat to take them to the steamer. How it was raining! Never before had the newcomers been in such a downfall as this. The floodgates of heaven seemed wide open, pouring forth rivers of waters. "It always rains like this in Singapore," they were informed.

They could understand now, the warning about malaria, and were glad to wait under cover for the boat, that was not there, to come; and for the sun, that was hidden, to shine again.

When at last the outgoing travelers were taken on board their steamer, and the missionary was returning in the boat with her one guest, all nature was smiling as if she had never been in tears.

"Just look at the English cathedral!" exclaimed Miss F. "What a grand sight!"

"But it's all covered with mold," said the little missionary.

"Yes, that's what makes it look so ancient and fine," said Miss F.

"How long has it been built?" asked the little missionary.

"Thirty years," was the reply.

CHAPTER X.

"I FORGOT to tell you about your bed last night. Did you try to get in it?" asked Miss Blackmore of Mother Nind in the morning.

"Yes, I looked a long time for the upper sheet before I concluded there was n't any," was the reply.

"We always make our beds that way, for we seldom need any covering; and if toward morning it grows damp and cool, a light blanket or shawl, we find better than a sheet," said Miss Blackmore.

"I was glad you told me it was safe to leave my doors open," said Mother Nind, whose fondness for fresh air did not grow less in Singapore.

"Yes, the doors opening into the upper veranda are always open, night and day. If you will notice, we have n't a bit of glass in this house. The

open doors let in plenty of light, and we never
want to shut out the air," remarked Miss Blackmore.

"Is it always warm as this?" queried the little
missionary.

"Yes, and warmer; for this is our coolest time
now, during the rainy season," she replied.

"I do n't wonder that every one looks so pale,
then," said the little missionary.

"Every one gets sallow here," said a new deaconess, who was dreading the time when her face
should lose its fair complexion. "You can see the
roses fade out of one's cheeks, they go so quickly."

After breakfast, which was served at nine
o'clock, Mother Nind and the little missionary
were invited to visit a Eurasian school, that had
recently been organized by one of the missionary
daughters. The school was conducted in a base-
ment that seemed, with its stone pavement, not unlike a cellar. The children, too, looked like cellar-
grown plants, their faces so thin and sickly, and
their breath seeming to come in gasps. Poor
things! They can not live in the sunshine. It
wilts them; and they do not flourish in the shade.

From this school the visitors were carried in
the *gari* to a Chinese school, where English is
taught through the medium of the local Malay
tongue. The people of this school presented a
striking contrast to the English and Eurasians,
looking healthy and well suited to their surroundings. Their costume, modest as the Chinese dress

is under all circumstances, was the extreme of simplicity and perfect adaptation to a tropical climate— pantaloons and loose jacket, fastened in front by corded loops and knots for the boys; and for the girls, a plain, straight skirt, and a long, loose sack, held together by ornamental pins at neck and waist, and sometimes a third between. Their clothing was all of cotton, and the embodiment of ease and comfort.

Singapore, sometimes called the "Chinaman's paradise," is one place where he has come to stay. Several generations of Chinese have grown up on the island, forming the most stable, wealthy class in the community. They speak the easy Malay tongue, and are eager to acquire a thorough knowledge of English, which makes a good opening wedge for missionary work.

From Teluk Ayer, the Chinese school, several Chinese homes were visited. Mother Nind was surprised at the richness of the interiors. She had seen few houses like these in Foochow, she said. In some of the homes little schools were held for the girls; for the more aristocratic Chinese parents will not allow their daughters to go to public schools like Teluk Ayer. The greetings were more cordial than those to which Mother Nind had become accustomed; for the Chinaman in Singapore no longer shakes his own hands, but has wisely adopted the English custom of shaking his visitor's hands. Chairs were offered them. Often they were of beautiful inlaid work, set stiffly against the wall and alternating with small tables, all ready for serving the indispensable cup of tea; and sometimes after the tea, a handful of jasmine petals was given to each guest, as a sweet odor of hospitality to bear away. In one of these houses lived Sin Neo, the first woman baptized in the Deaconess Home. She had suffered much persecution for her heroism, but her face wore the look of a victor. After giving each of her guests a cordial hand-clasp, with Miss Blackmore's aid as an interpreter, she began to talk to Mother Nind. At first, both waited for the interpretation; but that soon grew too slow a medium of conversation as they found themselves understanding, the one the Malay, and the other the English, by gesture only. Sin Neo compared her height with Mother Nind's, to show that the latter was the taller; then Mother Nind pointed to her shoes and Sin Neo's bare feet, to convince her that she was mistaken, that they were really the same height. On parting, Sin Neo gave her guest a hearty kiss, humbly requesting her to condescend to become her mother.

Two or three days later she was present, with many other Chinese women and children, at a reception given to Mother Nind at the Deaconess Home. Most of them came in *garis*; for they belonged to wealthy homes, which would have been forever disgraced if they had walked. They were dressed like the girls in Teluk Ayer, the brilliant jewels that gleamed from their breast-pins forming a strong contrast to the cotton garments thus held together. Their teeth and lips were stained with the juice of the betel-nut, which many of them continued to chew during the reception. But some of these stained lips moved a feeling response when Mother Nind said they should pray every day; and when she had finished her address, Sin Neo voiced their thoughts in a little speech, thanking her for coming, and expressing the wish that she might live to visit them again.

It was examination time in the Middle Road School for Girls. The platform and altar—for the school had to serve as a church on Sundays—were banked with palms. Bouquets of roses and ferns were ready to be given to the examining committee and visitors. The pupils were dressed as for a picture, each with a bit of her best sewing spread on the desk before her. At the appointed hour a carriage drove up, and Lady Mitchell, wife of the governor of the Straits Settlements, stepped out. She and a lady friend were the examining committee, and very carefully and thoroughly did they inspect each little piece of work. When they had finished, the school was called to order, and she arose to express her approbation, in a few sweet, gracious words; then the flowers were presented, and she was gone. The ordeal had lasted but an hour, and there was still time for singing and a talk by Mother Nind.

"How much better they sing here than in China or Japan!" she said to her companion on the way home. "Their voices, many of them, are really

sweet; but in China I often felt like putting my
hands in my ears when they sang."

"The Malay is a musical language, I think,"
said the little missionary, "and much easier than
Chinese.   In Shanghai I tried to learn a few
Chinese expressions; but I could not distinguish
the tones, and came away not knowing a single
word.   But in Singapore, already I have learned
several, and I love to say them."

On Sunday, Mother Nind and the little missionary separated to go different ways; for the
one had been asked to preach, and the other
wanted to see the Sunday-school work.   The latter came home very enthusiastic.   "Why, Mother
Nind! I thought I was a hard worker, and I
thought I had seen other missionaries work hard;
but Miss F. beats us all.   Since I left you at the
breakfast-table I have seen the beginning, middle,
and close of *eight* different Sunday-schools.   Three
of them were in the homes where we saw the little,
private day-schools; and the mothers and grand-
mothers stood around listening to the singing and
stories about Jesus with as much interest and attention as they gave to us and the English recitations
the other day.   One was a regularly-conducted
Sunday-school at Teluk Ayer, and the others were
street schools.   The teachers would station themselves under the shadow of a friendly roof, call
the children together by singing, show a picture
of the International Leaf Cluster, talk about it,
give them cards, and go on.   At one of these

CHILDREN OF THE HOME.

places the people invited us in, and said they would like to have the school inside next time. It is so different from our work in Japan!"

Mother Nind, too, was enthusiastic about her morning. She had a good time preaching to a mixed audience, with interpretation in Malay.

In the early evening there was a service at another Methodist church for an English-speaking congregation. The lamps were not yet lighted, though twilight, calm and cool, was rapidly stealing over the island of palms. Sweet odors pervaded the atmosphere; visions of dark, restful green, and soft, gentle blue filled every open door and window; the peace and beauty of nature had entered the "house made with hands." It was a communion service; and as the worshipers from far-away lands knelt at the altar, the good and true seemed never so near, and the bad and false never so distant, as there in wicked Singapore.

After the six o'clock dinner each evening, Sundays and week-days alike, the children of the Home came up the stairs to the drawing-room for a religious service. It was a curious family; dusky Tamils and fair Eurasians, Malays, Siamese, Portuguese—fit emblems of the heavenly home, which shall gather in its borders of "every kindred, and tongue, and people, and nation!" They sat on the floor with their feet crossed under them, and sang with great delight hymn after hymn; some in English, but more in the sweet Malay.

After they had gone one night, the little missionary said: "I'd like to see them at their meals some day."

"I do n't think you would enjoy that," Miss Blackmore replied.

".Why not? How do they eat?" were questions that quickly followed.

"With their fingers!" and both faces looked intense disgust.

"How much cleaner and more civilized chopsticks are!" thought the little missionary.

The Methodist work in Singapore was only ten years old; but in that one decade it had grown with tropical rapidity and in tropical variety. There was preaching in Chinese, as well as in Malay and in English; there were boarding-schools and day-schools; there was a Soldier's Home, an orphanage, rescue work, an active, busy press. One of the most flourishing institutions was an Anglo-Chinese school for boys, with an enrollment of six hundred students. Representing many different nationalities, the majority were Chinese. Coming from homes of wealth, they were able to pay for their education, and made the school largely self-supporting. Some of them were boarders, discarding chopsticks, and eating with knife and fork and spoon in approved European style. One day Mother Nind and her companion were invited to dinner in the boarding department, with the principal and his family. The dining-room was a large basement-room, another of the "cellars," as the little missionary

BREAKFASTING ON THE SCHOOL GROUNDS.

called them. The missionary, with his wife and children, sat at a table near the center. The vacant places at that table, as well as all the other tables, were filled with Chinese students. "This is wonderful!" exclaimed the little missionary. "I've never seen anything like it in Japan or China. The missionary eating with his pupils? We should starve on their food, and we could not afford to give them ours."

Mother Nind was invited to address the students at the school. She arrived before the morning session began, in time to witness a curious scene. Here and there, through the grounds, venders of various kinds of queerly-prepared food had planted their little stands; and the day-pupils, who had been their patrons, were standing near, eating their breakfast. Straw hats, felt hats, close caps, bare heads, shaven heads and cues, a strange mingling of the nations! But when they were called to order, and sang, in clear, ringing tones, and in the dear English words, "Gospel bells are ringing," it was clear how they were to be united: simply through the ties of the one true religion and the universal language!

"Will you come and take breakfast with us tomorrow?" was another invitation that came to Mother Nind and the little missionary. "How strange to be invited out to breakfast!" they thought. Early in the morning a cup of tea and bit of toast were served to them in the dining-room or in their own rooms, as they liked; but

the real breakfast was not prepared until nine or
ten o'clock, so that repast had grown to be as
much a company meal as any other. Often the
little missionary had looked out of her room, as
she was getting up, to see two of the missionary
daughters seated in an opposite veranda, poring
over their books with a teacher, trying to get as
much hard work done as possible before the heat
of the day began. When they came into their nine
o'clock breakfast, they had finished their Malay
lesson, and had done quite a bit of school-work
as well.

One morning the visitors were out before
breakfast. Every one had said they must not leave
without seeing the "Gardens;" so to the "Gardens" they went. And such gardens! Such trees,
such shrubs! Such luxuriance of foliage, such pro-
fusion of flowers! What envy they would arouse
in the bosom of a Northern gardener! He has to
labor so diligently in his greenhouse, with pipes
and hose and glass, to produce a few pots of green,
dwarfed, stunted specimens of the abounding mag-
nificence of the tropics, rejoicing if he be rewarded
now and then with sight of flower or fruit! There
was a place called a greenhouse in these gardens;
but it was only an open booth, destitute of glass, of
pipes, of hose; for the whole atmosphere is ever
steamy with heat and moisture, and the sun never
withdraws its warmth and brightness. They
would have lingered among the wondrous ferns
and orchids of that greenhouse; but the sun was

getting high, and they must hasten to the Home and breakfast.

One of the missionaries had a good story to report at table: " Many of the people who open their homes to the teaching of English are opposed to the Christianity we mix with it; but they think that while their children are little, it will not hurt them any. One man, lately, was much troubled because his wife had been listening and was inclined to believe. He said to some one: " My wife want to be Christian. I no like that; but she become very nice wife."

Luncheon was eaten in the home of the missionary who was engaged in rescue work. " There are a good many Japanese women here," she said to the little missionary. " Would n't you like to go out with me some afternoon to talk to them in their own language?" An appointment was promptly made. When the day and hour arrived, they rode in jinrikishas until they neared the dwellings of darkness. Dismounting, they dismissed the runners and walked to the one they wished to visit.

It was late in the afternoon. The women had just risen from their mid-day naps, and were engaged, some in dressing, and others in eating their evening meal. But all were quite ready to talk, and often indulged in a coarse, loud laugh at their visitors' expense. Tears came to the eyes of the little missionary. Could it be that these bold, brazen creatures in foreign costume belonged to the same race as the gentle, modest women, Christian and non-Christian, whom she had learned to love? She tried to appeal to that Japanese spirit, which so often outlasts the dying breath.

"Do n't you know you are a disgrace to your country?" she said.

"Kuni no koto wo sukoshi mo omoimasen (Our country's affairs we think of no more)," they replied.

"Do you see how rotten this wood is?" said a Singapore missionary to Mother Nind one day, as he put his foot down into great holes in the floor of his house.

"What makes it so?" she asked.

"White ants," he replied. "The only wood they won't eat is teak-wood; so that is almost priceless in value here."

The food in all the homes was kept from ants by inserting the legs of tables, sideboards, safes, and refrigerators in small vessels filled with water; but floors and ceilings could not be protected that way, unless, perhaps, the missionaries should adopt the Malay custom of building on piles over the sea.

At night lizards came out on the walls, frightening newcomers at first, but after a little becoming good company because of their quiet, unobtrusive, polite manners.

Day succeeds day, so hot and enervating that there seems to be only one good, comfortable hour in the twenty-four; and that is the hour of the daily bath. The bath-room is there; not a luxury

as in many American homes, but a positive necessity. It does not contain a beautiful porcelain tub,
with hot and cold water to turn on at will; it has
not even a Japanese hogshead, with a charcoal
stove inside to heat the water so much hotter than
the surrounding atmosphere that the latter will
seem cool by contrast. Its appointments are the
simplest possible—only a jar of cold water and a
dipper; but they are quite enough to give one the
most refreshing bath in the world—the cold shower-
bath of India and Malaysia.

"A week is a very short time to spend in Singapore," all the missionaries said to Mother Nind.

But their passage was engaged on the steamship
Lindula of the British India Line. A heavy shower
was threatening, as a few friends drove with them
to the steamboat landing; so good-byes had to be
hurried. As they saw the *garis* that contained their
friends moving rapidly away, and the first drops of
the threatened rain beginning to fall, Mother Nind
voiced the feeling of homesickness and loneliness
that came to them at the beginning of this new
voyage, by saying, "We seem quite alone now."
But in an energetic manner she shook it off at
once by making herself at home in her new surroundings, opening her traveling-bags, and neatly
disposing in her stateroom the various articles she
expected to need on the voyage.

They were out only a day or two, when the
steamer made her first stop at Penang. It was early
in the morning when she came to anchor; but

through the kindness of Singapore missionaries, some one knew of their coming, and was ready with a boat to take them ashore. This "some one" looked harassed, and was quick and nervous in manner. With her ready sympathy, Mother Nind soon learned the cause. In a climate where one man's work should be divided among two or three, he was, according to that ratio, shouldering the work of six. He was a physician with a considerable practice; as presiding elder of the Penang District, he preached each Sabbath in three languages—English, Chinese, and Malay—besides preparing to conduct sacramental services in Tamil, and was general superintendent of a number of schools taught in these various languages. When they arrived at his home, they found a school on the first floor, and an invalid wife and family of frail, delicate children above. A large room served for a drawing-room at one end and a dining-room at the other. The little missionary was captivated at once by the broad, beautiful sea-view from the windows. "How delightful!" she exclaimed. "I'd like to have a picture of it!"

A little later she remarked, "This beach must make a fine bathing-place for the children."

"They never bathe there," wearily replied the mother. "They can't on account of the sharks."

The little missionary looked aghast.

"But can't you protect a little place for them in some way?" she said.

"Yes, but it would cost a hundred dollars to do so," was the reply.

"I do n't believe I ever had any real trials," thought the little missionary. "Those I thought I had grow smaller and smaller as I see other missionaries, and will soon be gone entirely, I am sure."

After breakfast and prayers with the servants— a difficult task, as they represented almost as many different races and languages as individuals—their host proposed to take them out sight-seeing.

"There are the 'Gardens' and the schools. Where shall we go first?" he asked.

"O, the *work* must be first," quickly answered Mother Nind.

The schools, though not so numerous, presented much the same variety as at Singapore. Another big Anglo-Chinese school was trying to grow still larger in a small, inconvenient, rented building. A school for girls, giving instruction in Malay and English, did not yet aspire to the dignity of a building to itself; but was the one first seen in the missionary's home. A little school, swarming with black, half-naked Tamils, proved most interesting. Their chief instructor was an old man of their own race, who had become an earnest Christian, bearing the significant name of Simon Peter.

"Penang is larger than Singapore, and the heat is more trying because of the reflection from these white roads," was information given on their way to the "Gardens." But they did not mind the

14

heat and the reflection, for they had entered a cocoanut-grove. They never knew how far they drove through that forest of palms, but it seemed to extend miles in every direction. How they delighted in looking up at the feathery, graceful fruits about them! The fruit was fully grown, and they wondered how the big nuts could be gathered from the extreme top of those tall, slender trunks. But there was never any trouble about that, they were told. Not one, even on the tallest palm, was ever sacrificed, because it was hard to reach.

As soon as they emerged from the forest, they were in the heat again. It was too hot to enjoy walking about the Gardens, and they were content with one look at the mysterious waterfall, whose source yet remains unknown, but whose volume is sufficient to supply the whole city with water.

When, after a full day, their host took them back to the steamer, they found the hold just closing on a million cocoanuts, the cargo received since morning.

The following day at sea, as they were sitting below, all at once they heard unusual noises on deck, the rapid turning of the screw, then dead silence. The steamer had stopped in midocean! After a little pause they were relieved to hear the sound of the propeller again, and the ship moving steadily as before. Going on deck, they discovered the cause of the disturbance. A junk containing seven or eight people, one of them a woman, was lashed to the ship, rising and falling in the constant swell caused by the large vessel. Seventeen days before, she had started from Penang for the little island of Junk Ceylon, after a load of bullocks. One night, soon after starting, she had drifted from her moorings; and for fifteen days her unfortunate passengers had been wandering in the open sea, unable to get their bearings and determine their course. Once before they had seen a steamer and signaled their distress; but, like many other distressed travelers, had been "passed by on the other side." Rice and water were nearly gone, just enough for that one day; then they must lie down to die. But the *Lindula* was a "good Samaritan," who stopped on her journey, going fifty miles out of her course to take the wanderers toward their desired haven.

Provisions and water were given them; and as the water coursed slowly through the long hose into their barrel, the captain's voice rang out: "Fill her up *full*." Mother Nind whispered, "How like our captain that is!" Before the junk was cut loose, her captain, a native who could speak fairly good English, was called on deck and interviewed. He salaamed to Captain Withers, who said: "You have taken me out of my course. You must pay me a thousand dollars."

The poor fellow put his head on his breast and replied: "Me no money! Make me your servant forever!"

Captain Withers said: "Then I put your junk

on board with all our passengers, and take you to Rangoon to have you shut up in jail."

Quickly came the answer: "No do that! Cut my head off! That better!" And after a little pause, "But you no save me to kill me!" and all anxiety faded from his face, leaving it smiling and confident.

The sun was setting when the junk was cut loose, her captain vigorously waving his bandana, and all on board both boats bright and happy. Those on the big vessel watched with great interest as the little sail was raised and the junk began to move toward her port, which was then in plain sight; and they continued to look, until their own more rapidily moving steamer caused her to fade from her view.

The passenger list of the *Lindula* was longer than that of the *Formosa*, and included a number of second-class passengers. Mother Nind was much distressed to be the owner again of a first-class ticket. Two missionaries from West China were traveling second-class, and they tried to relieve her distress. They were in Chinese dress, with long cues hanging down their backs, and had thrilling tales to tell of the riots which had driven them from their work. "We are used to anything; second-class is good enough for us, but it would n't do for you," they said to her.

The first-class travelers included a niece of the Vanderbilts, on her wedding journey around the world; another lady traveling alone, except for

her maid; and several gentlemen. Among these
was an old man who had accumulated much
wealth as a tea-merchant, and who was distinguished as a member of the British Parliament.
He always spent the weeks when Parliament was
not in session in traveling; for, as he sadly remarked, "Though I have four houses I have no
home." Mother Nind and the little missionary
looked at him pityingly, as they quickly thought
of the many homes in India now waiting to receive them; of the homes where they had already
been so lovingly welcomed; and of the other homes
in far-away America, where their dear ones had
often looked and longed for them.

What a delightful inheritance they had in
houses and brethren, and sisters and mothers, and
children and lands! Had some fairy godmother
touched them with her wand? for they had suddenly
become rich while he was very poor.

Captain Withers, like most sea-captains, was
social and entertaining. Like many another, he
was attracted to Mother Nind, and often took a
brisk walk up and down the deck with her. "There
are two classes of passengers I never forget," he
said, "the nice ones and the nasty [pronounced
nähsty] ones. The indifferent ones, who sit off by
themselves reading, I soon forget; but I always remember the nice ones and the nasty ones." All
this, with an approving look at his companion, as
if he were already quite sure in which of his men-
tal classes she would appear! He took a fancy,

also, to the Chinese missionaries, and was enthusiastic in his remarks about them. "That Upcraft
is a wonderful fellow," he said. "I sat up in his
room until after eleven o'clock last night, hearing
him talk. Such experiences as he has had up there
in West China! Three times he had to escape for
his life in any kind of rafts or boats that he could
get to take him down the river. Sometimes the
wretches were determined to put him ashore; and
he had to save himself, and those with him, by
guiding the boat himself. Once they would all
have been killed if he had not fired off a rifle,
which he happened to have with him, because he
had just brought it out from America to give to a
Chinese friend who wanted one. I tell you he's a
hero, if there ever was one. The other one, too,
is just as brave, I suppose, only he has n't been in
it so long. And they 're both going back by way
of Burma, not a bit afraid, though they take their
lives in their hands as they go!"

Mother Nind herself often had long talks with
the brave young fellows, who were as gentle and
winning in their ways as though they had never
been compelled to face a Chinese mob; and when
she parted with them in Rangoon, it was, to her,
like parting with sons; and to them like saying
"good-bye" to their mother.

CHAPTER XI.

"THERE are the golden pagodas of Burma!" said Mother Nind. The little missionary had just come on deck, to find their steamer slowly approaching Rangoon.

"What kind of money is used in Rangoon?" was the business-like question of an American passenger near by.

They knew the answer, for Captain Withers had already posted them; and the little missionary had written in her pocket memorandum:

1 rupee = 16 annas.
1 anna = 4 pice.

"There are two-anna pieces, four-anna pieces, and eight-anna pieces," he had further explained. "Four annas will do for the coolies who take your luggage ashore, and eight annas for your *gari*."

Soon they were giving this address to a *gari* driver, through an officer who was going ashore and so kindly volunteered to interpret:

REV. JULIUS SMITH,
19 Lancaster Road.

Yes, he knew the place; and off he went. But he could not have known it; for after a little, he stopped in front of a photograph gallery, called out some one who could speak English, asked again for

215

the address, and drove on.   After awhile, they entered Lancaster Road.   "You look on that side of
the street for No. 19, and I will on this," said
Mother Nind. They drove to the end of the street,
but had not found it.   The driver turned back.
He hailed a passer-by, and inquired again.   Soon
he stopped in front of a house, and the little missionary got out.   " Does the Rev. Julius Smith live
here?" she asked.   The servant ushered her into
the drawing-room, where she waited for the lady
of the house to dress and come down.   " This is
the wrong Smith," she said.   " Rev. Julius Smith
lives over there."

At last they drove, not in front, or up to, the
house of the Rev. Julius Smith, but *under* his residence.   There it was above them, with plenty of
room beneath for a driveway, a playground, and a
carriage-house. It gave them a curious sensation
to get out of the carriage on the ground-floor of
the house, and at the foot of the hall stairs.   But
they had made no mistake this time; for a cheery
welcome was floating down the stairs, and the Rev.
Julius Smith himself coming in sight.

Mrs. Smith, they soon learned, was ill in bed;
but her warm-hearted hospitality would not allow
them to go elsewhere for entertainment, or their
visit to be marred in any way by her sickness.
That evening they were taken for a drive in a *tum-
tum*, after a little pony about the size of the Singapore ponies.   This *tum-tum* was an open dog-
cart with an extra seat, whose occupants were

required to sit with their backs toward those in the front seat. Their companion was a missionary daughter, who wore the simple gray dress with which they had become familiar in Singapore—the deaconess costume adopted by the Methodist Church in India and Malaysia. After talking with Mother Nind about the work for a while, suddenly she turned upon the little missionary: "There are sixty languages spoken in Rangoon! Which one of these shall we learn?" she asked.

Evidently she did not expect an immediate answer; for she soon remarked, in a lighter strain: "One of our visitors recently called this 'the prettiest drive in the world.'" They were going through an avenue bordered by shade-trees, over one of the smooth, good roads, which the English know so well how to make. The moon was up, enhancing them with flickering lights and shadows. Strains of music filled the air; for they were nearing the public gardens, where an English band played every evening. Soon the band-stand came in sight, and a number of people, apparently English and American, were strolling about the grounds. As they turned from them to the other side of the driveway, they saw the moon reflecting its brightness from the surface of a clear, beautiful lake; and the little missionary remembered what some one in Singapore had said to her: "There are three sights in Rangoon—the pagoda, the elephants, and the lakes."

In the morning, after the early tea and toast,

their host got out the *tum-tum* again to take them
to the great pagoda, called the "Sway Dagon," or
"Glorious Golden" pagoda.

There were four entrances; but they naturally
chose the most imposing, guarded by two colossal
stone lions, and began at once the ascent of the
two hundred and fifty-one steps leading to the ele-
vation on which the pagoda had been erected. The
way was bordered by booths for the sale of flowers
and other offerings to the gods. The fingerless
hands of lepers were extended for alms, exciting
in the little missionary's mind, she was sorry to dis-
cover, not the compassion which the Savior had for
such, but a feeling of intense loathing and disgust.

At last they had passed the long line of beggars
and of those that bought and sold, and were among
the worshipers on the broad stone pavement that
surrounded the golden pagoda. How different from
the pagodas of China and Japan, which were built
of wood, and could be entered and even ascended!
This was a solid mass of brick and earth, covered
only with gold. They differed in shape also, the
former being square and scarcely smaller at the top
than at the bottom; while the latter was round,
tapering to a slender spire at the top. No pagoda
they had seen before could equal this in size, in
height, in imposing grandeur. The base was ornamented throughout its entire circumference by
smaller pagodas, grotesque images, and kneeling
elephants in stone, forever paying their silent
adoration to the Great Pagoda.

"They have to keep renewing the gold-leaf," said Mr. Smith. "It peels off, and grows dull and dingy after a time. Do you see that bright band up there? That has been put on recently. The gold-leaf is sold at the entrance to worshipers, who present it as their offering to the pagoda ; and in that way it is kept in repair. I want you to notice what looks like an umbrella near the top. That is jeweled, and is worth thousands of dollars."

On the same level with the Great Pagoda was a circular labyrinth of inferior pagodas and shrines. The shrines were literally storehouses for gods of all sizes and many different materials, but each bearing the placid, smiling face of Gautama, the founder of Buddhism. The posture, too, with one exception, was the old, familiar one, with legs crossed in front; but not sitting on a lotus-blossom, as in Japan. There was one reclining Buddha, thirty feet in length, attended by stone priests, that there might always be some who were never betrayed into negligence in his worship. A large mango-tree was surrounded by shrines, which were ever cracking and needing to be rebuilt as the tree expanded. Some of the wood-carving was finely wrought, one piece especially arousing the admiration and wonder of the visitors. It was a doorway; and among the flowers and leaves, which formed a graceful border, several bullock carts were carved, so perfect and real in appearance that they seemed quite ready to descend and go about their work of drayage. The bells used in worship were very large, each occupying a special shrine, and of a full, rich tone, which, if Gautama could not hear, must delight the worshipers to produce.

"I can tell you a story about this one," said Mr. Smith. "When the English conquered Burma, they took possession of this bell, intending to transport it to England; but in shipping it, through some carelessness, it dropped into the sea. A noted engineer was sent for, and came all the way from England to raise the bell; but his best and most scientific efforts failed to get 'Humpty Dumpty' up again. Then the Burmans presented themselves before the English officials, and asked if they might try to raise the bell, and, should they succeed, if it might be theirs again. Permission was readily given; and with their rude native contrivances they accomplished what the famous engineer had given up as impossible. And now here it is in its old place by the Great Pagoda?"

They had nearly made the circuit, and stopped to watch the worshipers who were kneeling on the stones before the pagoda, with heads bowed and hands clasped in prayer. Priests with shaven heads, and dressed in loose garments of yellow silk, were here and there still engaged in eating their morning rice. Busy workmen were employed in making more idols. "Gods many, and lords many," involuntarily quoted Mother Nind. "Were it not for the promise that the idols shall all be destroyed, upon what could we pin our faith in the ultimate triumph

of Christianity?" That night she wrote in her
note-book, in her comprehensive style : "Grounds
covered with shrines and Buddha in various sizes
and postures, hundreds of them—brass, stone,
gold, silver, glass, bejeweled—with beds for him
to sleep on, couches to recline on, umbrellas to
shield him from the sun, chairs on which to sit,
curtains even of netting to protect him from mosquitoes!" As they descended the long flight of
steps by which they had entered, they heard music. Soon they saw the musicians, who were playing on cymbals and other more curious instruments, some of which were manipulated with both
fingers and toes. They were mourning the death
of a nun, whose body lay in a coffin near them.

On the drive home, the little missionary, who
sat on the back seat, found herself all at once high
in the air. She looked around, to see Mother Nind
and their host equally low. The little Burmese
pony had stumbled and was rolling about on the
ground in his harness. He succeeded in breaking
it, compelling them to walk the rest of the way,
and thus they had a little more of the freshness
and sweetness of the morning air between their
last sight of the lepers and breakfast.

Soon after breakfast they were whirled off again
in a closed *gari*, for it would not do to go out in
the *tum-tum* when the sun was up so high. They
stopped in front of a school-building. It had a
respectable air on the outside, but proved to be old
and decayed within. Its four walls included a large

day-school, with boarding and kindergarten departments, an orphanage, and homes for the workers in
charge of these institutions. So far as the trans-
mission of sound was concerned, all the rooms
were made as nearly one as possible by numberless
ventilators, transoms, and low screens serving as
doors. One of the missionaries aptly remarked:
"The houses here are made for air, and not for
prayer. I have no place where I can go to pray,
except the bath-room."

The children in the school and orphanage were
mostly of English and Eurasian parentage, and
looked frail and delicate, like those in Singapore.

In the kindergarten department they met a native of Ceylon, who was in training for work in
Singapore. She was the child of Christian parents, who had given her the name of Laura, which
sounded queerly enough with the family name,
Gunatilaka. As she spoke modestly of her plans,
her big black eyes and brown face shone with the
earnest purpose which later generations of con-
verts are sure, more and more, to conceive and
accomplish.

They were invited to stay and see some of the
kindergarten songs and plays. "How well they
do!" remarked the little missionary. "Where did
you learn kindergarten?" she questioned Miss W.,
who had charge of this also, as a part of her big
day and boarding school.

"I had a few days at Chautauqua. The rest I
have learned from books and magazines," she replied.

Mother Nind's questions were pertinent as ever:

"What is your greatest need?"

"Teachers who can teach."

"Do your girls get converted?"

"The boarders do."

They could not leave without stepping into the little Burmese school next door. As a souvenir of this visit, they each received a favorite hymn, penned by one of the pupils in the beautiful circles which constitute the Burmese alphabet.

In the evening there was a prayer-meeting in the English church. (The word English here, as in India and Malaysia, does not imply that it belonged to the Church of England; but is used to distinguish the Churches that have services in English, from those where the preaching is in the vernacular.)

The prayer-meeting was preceded by a teachers' meeting, a model for fine questioning and thoughtful answering, but greatly disturbed at the beginning by a company of *mourning* musicians across the street. One of the teachers slipped out, and soon the music ceased, not to continue again until the people began to pour out of the church from prayer-meeting. It was a curious prayer-meeting assembly. There were men and women, such as one usually sees in a prayer-meeting; the school had come in a body, even little ones from the orphanage; and there were a number of British soldiers. It was the last of November, the beginning of winter in other lands, and of what is called "the cool season" in Burma; still the night was warm; doors and windows were wide open, and a man stood outside pulling great punkahs further to fan the breeze, until even Mother Nind was convinced that the members of this Church would not fall asleep for lack of ventilation.

There were yet two days before their return to the steamer; so their host proposed a trip by rail to Pegu, a town in the interior, where a mission had recently been opened through the benevolence of a single Church in the home-land. It was a long time since Mother Nind had been on a railway train; so the sight of a locomotive again could not fail to give her a sense of satisfaction. But how somber and unfamiliar the coaches looked, with their windows protected, in Indian fashion, by a deep hood or awning, to keep out the sun! They had their tickets, and essayed to enter, but were stopped by the guard:

"This is the ladies' department, and the gentleman can not go in," he said.

"Then we 'll go with him," said Mother Nind.

But this did not please the guard. The ladies should stay there, and only the gentleman go in the other compartment.

"But we want to be together, so that he can show us the country," protested the ladies.

After a little, quite reluctantly he allowed all to go in the next compartment. Like the other, it was small, with room only for a few passengers besides themselves. One of these was a young

man, dressed in silk, in the simple Burmese style,
but speaking English so well that they suspected
him of some years of student-life in a mission
school. He conversed readily and with evident
pleasure, until reference was made to the worship
seen the day before at the pagoda. Then he looked
embarrassed; said he did not want to argue; that
his ancestors all went twice a month to worship
at the pagoda, and he was content to do the
same. But he did not seem contented, and soon
slipped away from a companionship suddenly
grown uncongenial, into the friendly retreat of a
neighboring compartment.

At the station in Pegu they were met by the
resident missionary with his *tum-tum* and a hired
gari. The visitors were put in the *gari*, and had
gone but a little way when they were invited to
"stop and see something interesting." Under a
temporary booth, affording slight shelter from the
sun, a great company of people were sitting, or,
rather, squatting on the ground, each with a bowl
in one hand and a spoon in the other, eating dain-
ties made of rice mixed with various mysterious
condiments. "This feast has been going on all the
morning. It is given to celebrate the consecration
of a young man, who is still in his teens, to the
priesthood. I was over here earlier, and saw the
gifts presented by his family to the priests. One
of them was a set of English encyclopædia, which
I would like myself, and they were all valuable.
And his priesthood may end in a month's time!

15

That 's the way they do in Burma—seem to think it 's the proper thing to consecrate every young man to be a priest; and then he can stay one or not, as he likes."

This explanation was given hurriedly and in bits, as they got out of the *gari*, looked around on the feasting assemblage, and were helped in again. Their next stop was at the foot of a hill, on which stood a simple, new cottage, with the fairest of pictures framed in its plain doorway. A young woman, dressed in white, bore in her arms a pretty child, the faces of both shining with pleasure in this welcome to the one they knew and loved best, with their new friends whom he was bringing to their isolated home. All the way up the path in the hot sun this picture charmed them, and they almost feared it would vanish with the first greetings. It did vanish, but only to appear again in other graceful scenes, as the fair young hostess offered "Grandma" (for her big German husband would call Mother Nind by no other name) the simple comforts of her little home. All the journey and sight-seeing of the morning had been accomplished without other breakfast than the early tea and toast; and it was high noon when they sat down to what seemed so improperly designated the breakfast-table. In "Grandma's" presence conversation drifted into home channels. "Do n't we wish our mother could come to see us?" their host said to his wife; and then he told a story: "There are just ten children in Ella's

family. One Sunday their minister preached a sermon on tithe-giving, which must have made a great
impression on the youngest; for when he got
home he said: 'Mamma, we have given just our
tenth, have n't we? For there are ten of us, and
one has gone to be a missionary.'"

Soon after breakfast Mother Nind retired for
her afternoon nap; but the little missionary could
not resist the temptation, hot as it was, to ride in
the *tum-tum*, and see a little more of a real Burmese village. The houses were so queer, built up
high in the air; and were less substantial even
than the famous "paper houses" of Japan. Just
a few bamboo poles and strips of matting—a shelter from the sun, with plenty of air, and no at-
tempt at privacy! She could look freely into
every home they passed, and see the men idly
sleeping away the hot hours of the day, while the
women were busy with their sewing and weaving.
"That is always the way here," said her companion. "The women do all the work, and the men
do nothing. I get thoroughly out of patience with
them, they are such a lazy set." Just then the little
missionary saw a man stop at a jar by the roadside,
help himself to a drink, and pass on. She looked
up questioningly, and he replied: "Some man here
in Pegu keeps that jar filled with water all the time,
as one way of winning the favor of the gods."
"Not a bad way of winning men's favor, it
seemed, on such a hot day, in such a hot
country!"

When Mother Nind came down from her nap she found some strange little guests waiting to see her. They were the pupils of the Burmese day-school. "Would she like to hear them sing?" "Yes, of course," she replied; and they sang for her the same sweet child-song which she had herself learned in English, and had so often since heard in Japanese, in Chinese, in Malay, and even in Tamil. Everywhere she went they sang that first, as if they knew and loved it; and surely the gospel could not come to them first in a better way than through the medium of

"Jesus loves me, this I know,
For the Bible tells me so."

As the missionary's wife watched the dark, shining faces of the little singers, her own assumed a beatific expression, and she remarked in a whisper, "Are n't they lovely?" The little missionary smiled. She had not thought of calling these children lovely; but she knew others, with just as queer faces and curious dress, to whom she would have applied that expression. "It must be," she concluded, "that we missionaries have the real mother-love, and so each thinks our own crows the whitest."

"Are these all boys, or all girls?" she asked, when they had finished. "They seem to be dressed just alike."

"O no! There's a difference," said Mr. S.; and he called one of the boys forward. His dress con-

A TAMIL GROUP.

sisted of two pieces; a short, plain jacket, and a straight piece of cloth tucked around the waist for a skirt.

" Dress yourself like a little girl," was the order given. Carefully he pulled out one corner of his skirt and brought it over smoothly and a little to one side, letting the end hang plain.

" Now like a boy again!"

Out came the corner of the skirt once more, to be tucked in its old place, which made the end fall in a deep flounce or ruffle directly in front.

" So it 's the women who do the work, and the men who wear the ruffles in Burma!" commented the visitors.

As soon as the children was gone, the *tum-tum* and *gari* were brought around, and all went out to see the school that had been opened for Tamil boys and girls. As a means of greater entertainment the order of exercises was varied at once by singing. Mr. S. remarked:

" I think Tamil must have been the first language God created in his fierce wrath at the Tower of Babel, the sounds are so harsh and difficult to distinguish."

Next an English class was called up, and some of the larger boys were asked to read. These dusky children of the tropics seemed to appreciate their varied accomplishments, and read eagerly, one after another, parts of the famous story of the " boy George, who received a present of a small ax from his father," etc. " Why does n't

it give his full name?" wondered the little missionary, until she looked at the title-page and discovered that it was an English publication.

The most interesting of all the exercises was
a native drill in calisthenics.   Each child bran-
dished two bamboo sticks, striking one, then the
other, then both together against his neighbor's,
swinging around with a jump, and a song, and a
dance, all rolling the whites of their eyes in enthusiastic delight, and continuing their weird movements for some time after the master had ordered
a halt.

In the evening Mother Nind was asked to talk
to the servants as they were gathered together for
evening prayers.   Her interpreted words were followed by prayers in Tamil, Burmese, and, out of
courtesy to her, in English also.

There was one "sight" still awaiting them in
Rangoon, which their friends would not allow them
to miss.   So good-bye to the little mission home
and work in Pegu; and in Rangoon once more on
the way to McGregor & Co.'s lumber-yard.

They stopped first at the home of one whom
Miss P. admiringly called "the biggest elephant of
them all," dear Father Brayton, pioneer of the Baptist Mission to the Karens, and in his earlier years
companion of the sainted Judson.   He was then
eighty-seven years old; and though he had given
over half a century of his life to the work, much
of it done in the jungles, he was still in "the
springtime of old age," as Mother Nind called it.

She asked for his autograph, and he stepped briskly across the floor to his desk in the next room. When he returned, he inquired in a sweet, gentle way, "How long have you been following the Master?"

"Sixty-five years," she replied.

"And I about seventy," he said.

For the little missionary's benefit, he gave some of his earlier experiences. "When my wife and I made our first trip up the river, crowds of people thronged the shores, and gathered about our boat whenever we stopped. This pleased us very much; but we thought it best not to 'write it up' until we had made one more trip. The next time scarcely any came. Their curiosity had been satisfied, and they cared nothing for our message."

Reference was made to his translation of the Bible; and he told how, as real success came to them in their trips up the river, he commenced this work; but for a long time he was unable to complete it, as he endeavored also to keep to his original plan of spending the whole of every dry season in the jungle, with his wife, in evangelistic work.

At last a company of native Christians came to him, and pleaded with him to finish the Bible. "If you do not finish it," they said, "we shall not have it at all; for it will take a new missionary too long to get the language to do it while we live. Please give us the Bible before we die."

Just then an attack of rheumatism made it un-
wise for him to return to jungle work; so he com-
plied with their request and gave them the Bible.

When the call was over, he politely offered his
arm to Mother Nind, escorting her down the stairs
to the waiting carriage beneath.

The afternoon was drawing to a close as they
reached the lumber-yard; but the elephants were
still at work. Quietly and with the real dignity
born of labor, they were moving about the yard;
the strongest, wisest, and best workmen were
there. No log was too heavy for them to drag
with their trunks; no plank was too thick or too
long for them to lift into the air, gently poising
it against their tusks until they had reached the
pile where it belonged. And when it came down
with a crash, no pains were spared in deftly pushing it this way and that, until the pile was left in
perfect neatness and good order.

Their movements were watched with intense
interest and admiration, and the visitors went
away, no longer wondering that such patient industry should be considered one of the "sights"
of the city.

It was Saturday night; and much to their regret, they had to return to their steamer, and spend
the Sabbath at sea. Among others to see them
off were the West China missionaries, who had
good news to report. At a little meeting which
they had addressed in a Burmese Church, the people were so stirred by what they heard that they

voted to give all the money in their treasury, about forty rupees, to the West China work.

This was a revelation of the budding possibil- ities of a Christianized Burma. In a land so rich in natural resources, and among a people so gener- ous, when at last the funeral dirge of heathenism is tolled, and the golden pagodas remain only as monuments to mark the burial, the light from the Christian spires will be shining out into *all the re- gions beyond.*

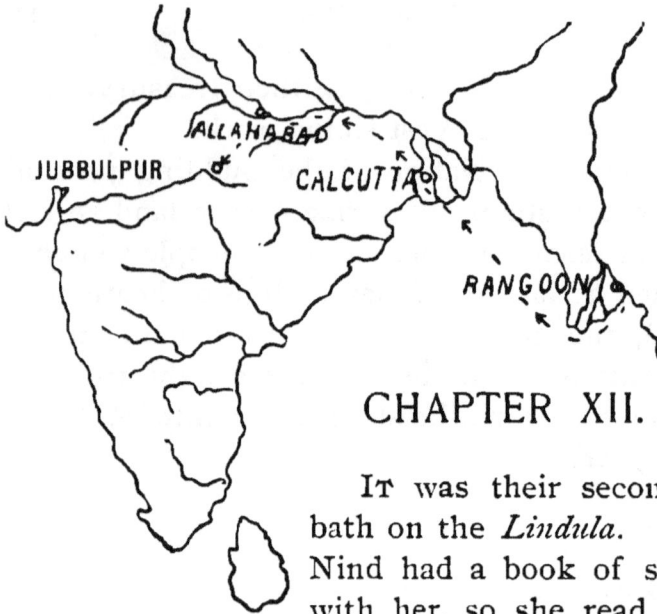

CHAPTER XII.

IT was their second Sabbath on the *Lindula*. Mother Nind had a book of sermons with her, so she read one to the little missionary; then the little missionary read one to her. That was their morning service. For their evening service they recited Scripture verses, each successive one beginning with the first letter of the last word of the preceding verse. The wonderful texts lost none of their significance in the little game, but seemed clothed with fresh grandeur, quoted under the " lesser light that rules the night," as it shone over the still waters of the Indian Ocean.

There were two or three days more of the "still waters;" then for three months they must exchange this quiet, restful sea-travel for the dirt and confusion and fatigue of railway journeys! As they thought of it, they felt loath to leave the sea, and lingered over each setting sun until its fiery splendor slowly faded from the last cloud; then down to dinner, and back to watch the moonlight, as though these glorious friends, also, would vanish with the sea.

They knew their steamer would make no delay, for she carried mail, and Captain Withers had told them what large subsidy she would forfeit if she failed to appear at the dock in Calcutta by such an hour on such a day. According to schedule time, on the fourth day out from Rangoon, she entered the Hoogly River. Her speed slackened, for this was the most dangerous part of her course. Already they could see rising above the water the two tall masts of the *Anglia*, which had been the last of the many unfortunate steamers to be entangled in the shifting sands of the treacherous stream.

"Most of her passengers were drowned just like rats in a hole," said the captain. "Their cabins filled with water, and the ports were too small for them to climb out. One man swam through the saloon to the deck, and was saved that way; but the rest were drowned."

After this story, what fascination rested in those slender, motionless masts! What warning for other ships! A little carelessness would make every mast like these; so who, out of port, could call himself safe?

There was delay at the landing in getting their trunks from the hold; and the day was fast turning into night when at last their luggage was all secured on the tops of two *garis*, and they were in-

side, Mother Nind in one and the little missionary
in the other, on the way to Dharamtala.*

They went first to the bishop's home, but no
one was there to receive them; then to the Deaconess Home. After some searching, they found
all of their Methodist friends together on the Compound of the Girls' School, enjoying a stereopticon
entertainment. The views were of Scotland, and
though it was difficult to journey to a land so re-
mote upon their first arrival in India, they did, at
least, enjoy the novelty of an open-air entertainment on an evening in December. Soon after the
last picture was shown, Mother Nind said "good-
night" to the little missionary; for she was to be
entertained at what she afterwards delighted to call
"the simplest episcopal residence she had ever
seen," while the latter was to remain in the Deaconess Home.

"Have you had dinner?" hospitably inquired
the superintendent of the Home.

The little missionary confessed that a cup of
tea and an English biscuit, taken before leaving the
steamer, were the only approach she had made to a
dinner.

"Then I must try to find something a little
more substantial for you than the rest of us have,"
said Miss M. A number of people had been invited to the Home for the late tea, which consisted
of bread already buttered and a cup of tea.

---

* Name of a street in Calcutta.

The search for something "substantial" resulted
in finding one egg and a little jam. "It 's a wonder
I found as much as that," she said. "Our cook
buys each morning just enough for the one day,
and so we never have anything left over."

Mother Nind had scarcely given herself one
night's sleep in Calcutta when she began to make
plans to regulate her first few weeks in India. She
engaged the bishop's wife and others in consultation; for, as she said, "I want to do what you think
best. Wherever I go I put myself in the missionaries' hands; for they certainly know a great deal
better than I what I ought to undertake in these
Oriental countries."

One week was reserved for Calcutta. It began
with a prayer-meeting in what was known, even on
the ships in the harbor, as "Bishop Thoburn's
Church." The Sunday congregations averaged
five hundred in the morning, and a thousand in the
evening; and the prayer-meeting had an attendance
of about three hundred. It was an English-speaking congregation; so Mother Nind could speak
without an "interrupter," as some one has called
the needful interpreter. During the singing of the
opening hymns the church filled with smoke. The
little missionary looked around in concern. But
every one was singing calmly, as if nothing were
the matter. She tried to follow their example;
but the smoke choked her, and she knew the fires
must be increasing. If no one else would give the
alarm, she must.

"What makes all this smoke?" she whispered to Miss M.

"O, it's just the evening fires of the people. The moisture keeps the smoke down," was the reply.

The little missionary had seen some of their fuel in a drive about the city that day. The "City of Palaces," she had found, contained more hovels than mansions. Often, under the shadow of grand, imposing English residences, she had seen rows of low mud huts, plastered over with cakes of manure, drying in the sun, and, down in the road, women and children gathering a fresh supply of the strange fuel with their fingers. And now, as they were using it to cook the evening meal, the air of the city was filled with the foul smoke. "What a trial it must be!" she thought.

After the prayer-meeting, quite a large company was invited to an informal tea at the Deaconess Home. This tea, following meetings at the church, was a regular institution, the newcomers were informed. It was the social net for catching strangers, and enabled the workers to draw more closely the influences of the meeting about many a poor prodigal thus brought within their reach. Often the tea became another prayer-meeting, as some wanderer, encouraged by friendly words, asked the prayers of God's people to aid him in leading a new life. The teas were not always at the Deaconess Home; but they alternated, sometimes at the parsonage, and often at the bishop's residence.

Mother Nind spoke not only at the prayer-meeting, but also, on Sunday, at both morning and evening services. For the first time in her travels in the East the woman-preacher was severely criticised by some that were outside, who expressed their comments through the medium of the morning paper. After preaching many times to Japanese and Chinese audiences, it remained for her own countrymen to quote St. Paul at length, and declare that she ought not to have been admitted to the pulpit. Only one woman before had been in a position to call forth such criticisms from the Calcutta press, and who was that other but her old friend, Amanda Smith?

Holiday vacation, which was the long one in the Calcutta schools, was approaching; consequently there were invitations for our travelers to the various annual exercises occurring before the close. First came the literary contest in the Girls' School, which was so able that every contestant seemed worthy of a prize. At the Prize Exhibition, which followed a few days later, gifts were bestowed upon the best pupils in all the grades of both this school and its large, growing offshoot at Darjeeling. So attractive were many of the prizes, which included dolls and trinkets for the younger ones, that it seemed quite like Christmas itself; and was, they were told, the nearest approach to a Christmas celebration in either of these large schools. The Darjeeling school had closed for a three months' vacation, which would cover the entire "cold season."

' That is queer," said the little missionary.
"Why do n't you teach during the cool weather,
and have your vacation when it gets hot?"

"O, Darjeeling is a hill station, so it 's always
cool there; and this is the only time in the year
when the children can really enjoy their Calcutta
homes," was the reply.

Both schools were boarding-schools. " We
have a hard time getting our scholarships taken in
America," said one of the missionaries. " It costs
so much more to support these girls than it does
the natives; and then every one seems to think
that the real missionary work, while this does not
count. But I am sure it does count; for some of
the girls who go out from our school make our
best workers, and most of them do go out to work."
They accompanied her in a call at the home of one of
the very poor Eurasian girls in the school. The family lived up-stairs in two small rooms, with scarcely
chairs enough to offer the three callers. The father
was out of work, and she was doing without a servant, which made living up-stairs very hard for her,
were the chief facts they learned from the mother,
who seemed to regard a servant as the great necessity of life.

" Even the poorest of those who have a little
English blood in their veins think they must keep
one or two servants. It is very hard for our girls
to be brought up in such a dependent way," said
their companion, as they drove away with this new
picture of poverty in their minds.

The boys' school for English-speaking students presented a similar problem of aristocratic, though dependent feeling. In the management of the school this feeling had been gratified to the extent of classifying the boarders; those who could pay little or nothing for their board, receiving less and called second-class boarders ; while those who could pay more, received better fare and were placed in the first-class. The scholarship boys, of course, were all in the second-class. One who was supported by private subscription suddenly became the recipient from home of an allowance, amounting to several rupees. Saying nothing to his benefactor of his good fortune, he paid the difference between first and second-class board into the school treasury, and was enrolled as a first-class boarder.

One of the missionaries who had gone out under the Woman's Society had somehow been attracted to the work of this school, and was engaged in the stupendous task of "mothering" all the boarders, investing their daily living, as far as possible, with sweet home and religious influences. She had the mother-instinct of self-denial, often forgetting herself so completely as to be without the necessary postage, even to send a letter to America.

A companion school for native boys was undergoing another kind of "hard times," as a favorite teacher was drawing many of the students away into a new school of his own.

The Bengali work for girls and women was in charge of one who, in addition to her busy cares as a wife and mother, gave enthusiastic, devoted attention to a large girls' school with a new boarding department, a normal training-class, and her zenana visiting. This school presented fresh novelties in dress and manners to the eyes of Mother Nind and the little missionary. The latter once asked a Calcutta missionary, who was seeking health and strength in Japan, if she had an Indian costume with her. "Why, it's only a strip of cloth," she replied. Here was the strip of cloth, the long, graceful *sari*, wound around the waist first for a skirt, then thrown over the head like a shawl or veil. Much the same kind of jewelry was worn as they had seen on the Tamils, who were also natives of India—nose-rings, ear-ring, necklaces, bracelets, anklets, etc. Just at the parting of the hair on the foreheads of some of the girls was a bright red spot. "That shows that they are married," said Mrs. L. Such little maidens to be wives—of nine, eleven; surely the oldest could not be thirteen! "I have myself known wives to be widowed at eleven," said Mrs. L. again.

The zenana women had a very low opinion of the little missionary when they learned that she had not been married. "Poor thing!" they said pityingly. "She can not get a husband!" Mother Nind satisfied them better as a visitor; for they could say to her, as they did to Mrs. L.: "You are just like us. You have a husband and children, so you can understand us, and we can understand you."

One of the deaconesses had a little Hindustani

school, which presented a fine picture of missionary beginnings. The building was a small hut, made of mud, with two or three openings left for windows. The only furniture it contained was one chair for the teacher; and a tin box held all the books and apparatus used in her work. The children sat on the floor, their black knees and toes sticking out in every direction. Their hair was uncombed, their bodies half clad, great hoops hung from their noses; and altogether they hardly looked like pupils of the fair-faced figure above them in her neat, gray dress and white apron. But no teacher in large, airy school-room, with slate blackboards, beautifully polished desks, and perhaps a piano, could look happier than she. With a hand laid tenderly on the black shoulder of a child just recovering from fever, and a look of love and pity for all, she stooped to their level, and taught them, patiently and simply, for Jesus' sake.

The visitors were fortunate in having an opportunity to attend the monthly Conference for missionaries of all denominations at work in Calcutta. It was the Methodists' " turn " to entertain, which means that they provided a meeting-place, also light refreshments to serve at the close of the Conference. The address was given by a convert from Brahmanism, who had belonged to the famous order of the " scarlet thread."

His subject was " The Trend of Modern Religious Thought Among the Higher Classes of India." It was an able lecture, delivered in faultless English; and while it dealt with philosophies which few of the missionaries present felt prepared to discuss, it encouraged them by showing the influence of Christianity upon the exponents of other religions. He had with him an "Imitation of Krishna," arranged with portions for every day's reading and meditation; but the vague, dreamy speculations which he read as the verses for the day, showed that only form had been copied; that the spirit of the living religion could not vivify a dead one—it must displace it.

One of the most helpful meetings of the week was a Saturday morning "believers' meeting." It might quite as well have been called the "doers'" meeting; for it was attended mostly by workers, some of whom were so busy with work in the vernacular that they had time for no other English service. Mother Nind was so busy helping in the various meetings that the little missionary had to go without her on an excursion to Serampore, where Carey first found a "cradle for Indian missions," under the protection of the Danish Government. The "Black Hole" remained unvisited by either. But one morning early they were ready for a drive to the "Gardens" across the river. After a little delay waiting for the *gari*, it came; a basket containing their breakfast was placed inside, and they started. Through the city streets, already alive with turbaned heads and bare feet; across the pontoon bridge, the longest in the world, some one said; rattling along a weary, dusty road, as the main avenue was closed for repairs,—at last they came to the "Gardens."

"Nothing looks well now, it is so dry," was the apologetic introduction of their friends. But, even with the memory of Singapore fresh in their minds, they knew nothing that could exceed the majesty and beauty of the wonderful avenue of royal African palms, which was just then opening before them. A little later they were out of the *gari*, walking toward the special object of their visit. It looked like a forest containing hundreds of trees. How difficult it was to believe that they all started from one trunk! Still they could see it was not a forest; for though it rose from level ground, it was pyramidal in form; and, as they entered, they could trace the great branches that went out from the central stem to form the first circuit of trees, and from these to form others. At the outermost circle, man's art had evidently been engaged in the work of rooting fresh branches in the ground, thus increasing the size of what was already known as "the largest banyan-tree in the world." "Almost every one walks around the tree to see how long it takes. It is usually called a seven minutes' walk," they were told. So Mother Nind and the little missionary started out, with watches in hand. They walked briskly at Mother Nind's best pace, and found they could do it in three minutes. Then, in the shade of the great tree, which might easily have sheltered a whole summer school or camp-meeting, they breakfasted on plantains and sandwiches.

Another morning, just after *choti hazri* (the little breakfast), they drove to "Kali Ghat," a bathing-place on the Hoogly, named for *Kali*, the patron deity of Calcutta. It was one place in India where animal sacrifices were still offered, and they came hoping to see the morning sacrifice; but were told upon arrival that it was not quite ready. During the waiting time they walked about the temple grounds, seeing sights that thrilled them more even than the shedding of blood. With feet crossed under them, some on the steps going up to the temple, others on the ground, were a few of the fakirs or "holy men," of whom they had so often heard. Their hair lay in matted, brown tangles, showing years of neglect; their clothing was in rags; their nails were claws; their faces wore a miserable, unhappy expression, which led Mother Nind to exclaim, "They look anything but holy!" Not far away was a group of lepers. Here one of the party tarried to drop a little money in each poor mutilated palm, saying compassionately, "I never can refuse to give these something."

Passing many other afflicted ones—the blind, the halt, the poor, the aged—they came to the "sacred well." It was surrounded by women, who were engaged in such unwomanly worship that the observers soon turned aside, speaking to each other only in low, hushed tones of what they had seen. As the sacrifice was still not ready, they asked the priest if they might look at the image of the goddess.

At once such a stormy altercation ensued that they would have ended it by leaving. But Mr. W. urged them to remain, saying that it was something they ought to see; so they waited. At last the party who wished to show the idol triumphed, and the doors were opened, disclosing a more hideous image than any Mother Nind and the little missionary had yet been horrified to behold. The light was too dim for them to grasp the details; but it seemed to be bathed in blood, with a long, blood-red tongue protruding from the mouth. They had to trust to other observers for knowledge of its black face; its four arms, one of them holding a scimiter, the other grasping a giant's head by the hair; its ornaments consisting of the figures of dead bodies for earrings and a chain of skulls for a necklace. But they had seen enough to make them anxious to get through the sacrifice, and away from all these vile scenes.

"Why are you so late with your sacrifice?" inquired Mr. W. Several times before he had asked this question, to receive always the answer that it would be ready soon. Now they replied that they could not offer the sacrifice unless Mr. W. would pay for the sheep. The visitors hardly cared to see sacrificing done to their own order; so they contented themselves with a look at the block where the animal was to have been offered, and went at once to the river side. Standing at the top of the long flight of steps leading to the water, they watched the bathers. Some, more richly dressed than the others, descended to the lowest step above the water, washed their feet, and returned; but others, after bathing their feet, their hands, their heads, immersed themselves, washed their garments, rinsed their mouths, and carried a vessel of the foul water, which they called holy, away with them.

One woman stood out of the water, apparently worshiping the sun; but all at once she turned and worshiped toward the south, then toward the west, and at last to the north. "She thinks she 'll hit it somewhere," said Mother Nind.

On their return, they stopped at a bank, and the little missionary went in to draw some money. She wished eight pounds; but when they brought the equivalent—one hundred and thirty-seven rupees, each the size of a silver half-dollar—she thought some one had made a mistake. Looking from the pile to her purse, and from her purse to the pile, at last she summoned courage to ask for a paper or a strong envelope; but they had already brought her a red bag with a yellow string, and into this she deposited the money; then clutching it in her hand she went into the street, miserably conscious that every one must be looking at her and her bag of money.

They were to start that night for Jubbulpur. Every one travels at night in India, and yet there are no sleeping-cars. When the little missionary went to the bishop's home in the early evening to see if Mother Nind was ready for the journey, she found her "doing up" her shawl-strap, rolling in with her shawl and pillows a blanket and light comforter. "I forgot to tell you that you would need bedding," said Miss M. to the little missionary. "You must have a *resai* [light comforter], too." The little missionary was not over-fond of packages, and was dismayed to learn that she must increase her hand-luggage by adding a comforter thereto.

At the station she discovered that nobody in India traveled in the American way, with a neat, trim valise and good, stout trunk; but every one seemed to have a great roll of bedding, and boxes, and baskets, and bags, *ad infinitum.* All these were tossed into the passenger coaches, and after them light tin trunks, until there was so little room left for the passengers that they had a wedged-in appearance as if they, too, were parcels. Mother Nind and the little missionary, not knowing the ways of Indian travelers, asked to have their trunks checked; and though one was only a hat trunk and the other a steamer trunk, both were over-weight, and required the payment of "excess" charges. They were to travel in the ladies' compartment of a second-class carriage, the bishop's wife and her little boy their only companions. As soon as they had started, with the good-byes of their Calcutta friends still ringing in their ears, they drew the shades, spread the *resai* on the seats for mattresses, and over them the blankets and shawls for coverings, thus preparing to spend as comfortable a night as possible on a train without air-brakes, which shivered and seemed to be going down a thousand embankments all at once every time it stopped. It grew chilly toward morning; and, in hot, hot India, they were glad to draw blankets and shawls close about them to protect them from the cold.

In the morning, station venders furnished them with tea for their *choti hazri;* and at nine o'clock they breakfasted from the big lunch-basket which the bishop's wife had thoughtfully prepared. Early in the afternoon they reached Allahabad, where they had planned to break their journey by a rest over Sunday. "Coolie hai!" called out their welcoming host, and soon their luggage was walked off on the heads of tall, well-formed coolies to a *gari* on the other side of the station.

"Our one guest-room is occupied by Miss B., of the Friends' Mission, who has been with us for some months," he said, when they reached the house. "But there is one vacant bed in that room; and we have put up a tent in the yard, which is at your disposal. So just arrange yourselves as you please," he continued. Later, another guest arrived, and promptly a second tent arose for his accommodation, until the ground between the home and church seemed quite like a piece of a camp-meeting. The resemblance was still more striking the next day, when the air was filled with songs of praise. The church was used by both English and Hindustani congregations, and with the Church and Sabbath-school services of each, there was as little time when no meeting was in progress as on any real camp-ground.

At one of the Hindustani services the preachers, pastor-teachers, and Bible-readers present received an informal introduction to Mother Nind, which consisted in standing in their places as their names were called. Then some of the children in the boys' school were brought forward and introduced as follows: "This child was found in a village street the other day, almost starved to death." It was not a time of widespread famine; yet what a thin, wan face; what tiny, shrunken arms! Another child was pushed to the front. "This child was just like him a year ago, but see how fat and plump he is now!" Then another: "This one was a wild boy from the jungles. When he was first brought to the school he would not wear clothes, nor sleep on a bed." And still another: "This boy was a little street Arab, who amused himself at first by running away." "Do you want to run away now?" he said to the child, who promptly responded with a negative reply.

Then, at a word, all sang with might and main the ringing *bhajan*, "Jai Prabhu Yishiu" (Victory to Jesus), and Mother Nind left to prepare for the evening service, where she rejoiced to see many of her English congregation around the altar at an after meeting, seeking the blessing of a "clean heart."

CHAPTER XIII.

THE Bombay Conference, which sat at Jubbulpur that year, was one of the younger Indian Conferences. Its members were mostly missionaries;
and so the business could be transacted in English
without interpretation. This made its sessions
more intelligible to Mother Nind than others she
had attended in the East. Though the Conference
was young, it contained members who had given,
some twenty, others thirty years to the service.
There was quite a break between these and the
younger men, who were. many of them, passing

through their testing time, trying to prove to themselves and others that they had not undertaken a
task too great for them; but that they could endure the climate, master the language, understand
the people, overcome the difficulties, be tactful,
brave, and hopeful under all circumstances.

The Woman's Conference was quite informal.
most of its reports being given orally. Like many
such, they were accompanied with alternate smiles
and tears. The Deaconess Movement had entered
the Conference during the year through one of its
opposers, who had, after a long, hard struggle,
joined this inner circle of consecrated workers, re-
nouncing half her salary, and donning uniform of
gray. Her sacrifice had brought another missionary to the field, and the two together were about
to engage in itinerating evangelistic work.

There was one cloud, heavy and dark, which
brooded over the entire Conference, marring its otherwise bright, sunny sessions. It was not the cloud
of failure; it was not the cloud of coming famine.
It was a cloud that had been gathering for some
time in far away America, and had now seemed
ready to burst over their heads—the cloud of finan-
cial depression! The bishop had been in the
States as usual, endeavoring to gather money for
the work; but he had no large collections, and only
a few special gifts to report. An increased appropriation for salaries of missionaries, allowed by
the Missionary Committtee, brought not a ray of
sunshine through the cloud; for that meant a cor-

responding decrease in the appropriation for native
workers.   There was only one hope, a hope that
seemed fast approaching realization before the eyes
of the visitors.   As the rains of adversity fell, they
would refresh the soil and make it more fruitful.
The greater the stringency, the more consecrated,
self-sacrificing, prayerful would the missionaries
become, and the less of a following would they
have for gain.

The members of the Conference and their
guests were entertained in three homes, one of
which was occupied for the occasion.   Five times
each day they gathered around the table for the
little breakfast, the big breakfast, the tiffin, the
dinner, and the tea.   "Don't tell any one how
many meals we have!" said the hostess, who remembered her "bringing up," and felt ashamed of
these adopted Anglo-Indian customs.

"But you have only two meals a day," said the
little missionary.   "The rest are just lunches."

"That's so!" she said, with a relieved look.

The room, occupied by Mother Nind and the
little missionary, opened into the back veranda;
and every morning, as they looked out, they could
see a tall, heavily-turbaned man-servant engaged in
his daily task of churning.   His churn was a small
earthen jar, containing fresh buffalo's milk.   A
bamboo stick, split at the lower end into four sec-
tions, served as a dasher, and was ingeniously
worked by means of a string attached to one of the
veranda posts.   The butter was served as it came

from the churn—a soft, white paste, with neither the milk worked out nor salt worked in—and some people liked it.

No sooner are the appointments read at a Conference than people begin to hurry away. Mother Nind's party was among the first to leave, as it included the bishop this time; and he was always in a hurry. He was hastening now to reach Calcutta before Christmas; and was planning then to have one whole week at home with his family. They averaged not more than six weeks together during the course of a year, his wife had said.

As they parted at Allahabad—for Mother Nind and the little missionary were to spend their Christmas in Lucknow—they accepted the loan of another blanket. Not only on the trains, but wherever they went, they needed plenty of bedding; for the guest-rooms of most of the mission-homes contained only empty *charpoi* (low, single beds made of four bars of wood connected by broad tapes, crossing and recrossing from side to side and end to end, the whole set upon four short legs, and making the cheapest of beds that can be called comfortable). The " cold season " in India was thus far an anomaly. In Jubbulpur the little missionary had been obliged to buy flannels for extra underclothing; and yet, at the same time, she had purchased a broad sun-hat of pith, and put a white cover on her umbrella, to keep off the sun.

Every one said that she must, that she would get a " touch of the sun " if she did n't; and ever since she had been in India, if a gleam fell across her face or shoulders, there was a sudden move- ment to shut it out; and if it happened to fall upon the back of her neck, there was great alarm; for "that is the worst place," they said. Mother Nind had come from Foochow, already prepared with her hat and umbrella for these attacks of In- dia's great foe; yet she had been ill in Calcutta from exposure in the Gardens; and the little mis- sionary herself remembered a severe headache that had kept her in bed part of one precious day in Rangoon. It was wise to be careful and shiver, if need be, in the effort to keep out the sun. But how she loved to dilate upon her glass-inclosed veranda in Hirosaki, and how the warm, bright sunshine, in which she could sit day after day with- out other thought than of comfort when asked, " Do you have to be careful about the sun in Japan?"

Another question usually asked her at the table, when there happened to be a lull in the con- versation, was:

"Do you have curry in Japan?"

Curry, made as hot as red peppers could make it, was a favorite dish in all the mission homes; and it was considered highly necessary, too, in en- abling one to resist the greater heat of the atmos- phere. If a new missionary did not like curry, older heads were shaken in solemn warning, as some remarked, " She 'll not be long for India!" A still better relish, called *chutney*, was highly

"EACH CRUMBLING TOWER."

esteemed. Mother Nind usually asked for sugar and milk with her rice; but the little missionary liked the curry, if it was not too hot, and she could eat the *chutney*, after she learned to take it in as infinitesimal quantities as freshly - grated horseradish.

They were accompanied from Allahabad by one whom the little missionary soon named the "grand old man" of the North. His wife and another lady were at the station in Lucknow to receive them. As soon as their faces were recognized by Mother Nind, her heart overflowed in an aside to the little missionary: "The *mother* of our Woman's Foreign Missionary Society, and our *first* missionary." The "first missionary" bore them away at once to the Woman's College. Her home was in an old Indian building, with such high ceilings and thick walls that, as they entered the great drawing-room, they seemed to be inside a church or cathedral; but a bright fire, burning in a grate at one end of the long room, soon gave them home comfort and cheer.

The next day was filled with preparations for Christmas. To the younger teacher was given the task of making sweets, and preparing great platters full of sandwiches; and the last thing at night, after the others had finished their work, the "first missionary" herself was found engaged in tacking up greens in the drawing-room and filling it with chairs.

Christmas morning early, while it was yet dark,

Mother Nind and the little missionary were aroused by the sound of singing. The English congregation had gathered in the drawing-room for their six o'clock Christmas prayer-meeting. This was a special Lucknow institution. There were always two of them, one for the English Church and the other for the Hindustani Christians. At the close of the prayer-meeting, sandwiches and coffee were served, greetings were exchanged, and the people dispersed.

At nine o'clock, before the real breakfast, there was a preaching service in the Hindustani church; and at eleven, just after, Mother Nind was to preach to the English congregation. It was rapid work going from one meeting to another, with a little breakfast in between; and she was quite too tired in the afternoon to accept an invitation to a Christmas-tree at the hospital of the Church Missionary Society. The little missionary went, however, and saw the patients, who were mostly women brought up in the dwarfing atmosphere of the zenana, huddled about their brightly-lighted Christmas-tree, seeming like little children in their pleasure and eager desire for gifts.

In the evening, the Lucknow missionaries and their friends, twenty-seven of them, gathered about one board for their Christmas feast. While they were partaking of a dinner which would have graced a festive occasion in any land, one of the guests said to another, " Do you realize that we are eating in a tomb?" " Yes," he added, " this is a

A HOME IN A TOMB.

Mohammedan's tomb, and the man who owned it is buried in the next room. It's a fine building though, and makes the best missionary residence in Lucknow."

It *was* a fine building, and the outer courts of the tomb had been so tastily converted into a dining-room, with a few other necessary living rooms, that no one would have suspected its original design.

The next day the travelers were entertained at the home of the " Mother of the Woman's Foreign Missionary Society." She showed them a precious little album, which contained photographs of the women who, with her, on a certain rainy day in Boston, started the organization, which they had lived to see grow beyond their wildest expectations. It was like looking at a tiny mustard-seed after beholding the great tree in whose branches they had so often lodged; and their hearts were filled with praise as they drove away at night, trying in vain to keep their *gari* closed against the evening smoke, which a heavy dew had made unusually dense.

They had other things to think of that night; for during the day they had been entertained by a drive about the city, which gave them glimpses of three of its attractions—the residency, the museum, and the public gardens.

The gardens were beautiful in tropical glory, in spite of the long drought; the museum was a study in the life and art of Oude and the surrounding provinces; and the residency was an in-

spiration, because of the thrilling story written
all over its ruined walls. Each crumbling tower
and jagged hole told of rebellion; each waving
flag, of victory; each clambering vine, óf peace!
Each·sheltered grave in its lovely grounds spoke
of wounds, of disease, of famine; each monument, of heroism, of faithfulness, of martyrdom;
but it was left for one underground room to tell
the saddest tale of all—the tale of patient waiting.
During the long, weary siege of Lucknow, this
dungeon-like place was the only refuge for the English women and children; and within its not altogether safe walls, they were kept, two hundred and
seventy-five in all, for six months, unable to fight—
waiting, simply waiting for release or death.

The missionaries, who were planning Mother
Nind's time for her, said she must see the first Industrial Exhibition of the Christian Association
at Cawnpore. They had passed Cawnpore on the
way to Lucknow; but it was only a short journey,
and there were many Lucknow missionaries going
with them to attend the Convention. They traveled in what was known as an intermediate compartment. On Indian railways, caste distinctions
are indicated, not only by first-class, second-class,
and third-class compartments, but there are ladies'
reserves, zenana carriages, carriages for soldiers,
and, between the second and third-class, an intermediate compartment. Theirs was still further
distinguished by a ticket marked, "For Europeans
Only."

This helped them to understand an anecdote told by the "grand old man" at the Convention.

"An Indian dressed in European clothes, was seated in a railway carriage marked 'For Europeans Only.' A Scotch woman came along, took a good look at him; then read aloud 'For Europeans Only,' and, turning to him again, called out, 'Come oot o' that!' Now," continued the speaker to his audience of young Indian Christians, who were inclined to think of European dress and customs as a small boy thinks of the first suit that is to distinguish him from a girl, "do n't be ashamed of being an Indian! Wear a European coat if you like, but do n't think of that as making you a European!"

Then he told the story of a young Indian who not only pretended to be a European, but made his father serve as his coolie, until one of his aroused hearers expressed the feeling of all in a cry of "Shame!"

Several of the Indian members of the Association gave addresses, some of them in good English, with only now and then a slip in pronunciation, or an amusing order like "Open your ears and hear wide!"

The industrial exhibits were disappointing in containing very little purely native work, but were good copies of European needlework, embroidery, carpentry, bookbinding, leather work, etc. Besides the medals and prizes awarded to exhibitors, two others were offered to winners of scholastic

honors. The recipient of one of these was a
teacher in the Woman's College at Lucknow,
Miss Lilivata Singh, the first woman to take the
M. A. degree at the Allahabad University.

It was an exciting time for the native Christians in Cawnpore, as some of them were also saying farewell to Dr. and Mrs. H., who had been for
many years their special friends and care-takers.
They made speeches to them, and sang songs for
them; they put their gift of an Indian coat on the
Doctor, and clasped a showy chain of silver about
the neck of Mrs. H., besides adorning her with
garlands of flowers; and at the last they brought
out refreshments, which consisted of cups of strong
tea and curious cakes, fried in grease; not nearly
so palatable as Japanese sweets, the little missionary declared.

The girls' high school was closed for the holidays; so Mother Nind and the little missionary saw
only the few boarders whose homes were too distant for them to visit. One of them was a little
girl, named Isabella, who had a very hot temper.
Quite recently she had "given her heart to Jesus,"
and had seemed much improved; but on one of the
idle days, when "Satan finds some mischief still,"
another girl had struck her. Instantly the old fiery
temper was aroused, and when their teacher appeared she found them angrily at work pulling
out each other's hair. This suggested their punishment, which consisted in cutting off all their
hair and sending them to bed; and when the vis-

itors were taken through the long dormitory, there were the two shamed children lying on their beds in broad daylight, their hair in two small heaps on the floor.

"The Eurasian children are so passionate! I think that good Christian schools are needed for them quite as much as for the natives," said the teacher, and her guests assented.

"I have just an hour in which to take you to the cemetery, Memorial Well, Memorial Church, and Massacre Ghat; but I think I can manage it." This remark came later in the day, as they were re-turning from the closing session of the Convention; and she did manage it—the bright, wide-awake young missionary, who had been looking and longing for Mother Nind even before she was laid aside for many weary months with fever, not knowing whether it was death in India or return to America that the Lord had in store for her. There was just one grave, a missionary's lonely grave, which attracted them to the cemetery; and standing by it they recounted its story once more. "She was taken ill at the dinner-table one night, and the next evening her body lay here."

They found Memorial Well surrounded by a beautiful park, into which none but Europeans are ever allowed to enter. A silent white angel, with folded wings, marks the spot where Havelock and his soldiers found the mangled bodies of massa-cred English women and children, many dead, others still breathing; and inclosing the well is an

imposing, handsomely-carved wall of stone. As
they were descending the steps of the inclosure,
Mother Nind's heart turned from sympathy for the
dead to interest in the living; and she said to the
young soldier who was serving as their guide, "Are
you a Christian soldier?"

He looked embarrassed, but finally stammered
out, "That's a hard question to answer!"

"If you're not, you ought to be," she continued.

"That's what my old father used to tell me!" he
replied.

"And now this old mother tells you!" said she.

"It's too hard work to live a Christian life in
the service. I try to do the best I can," he argued.

"But it isn't easy to do the best you can, without the Lord to help you," she urged.

There was a pause, as a good Spirit, fairer and
holier than the one over the well, strove within;
then in an ordinary tone he said:

"Would you like to see the place where the
house stood, in which the massacre occurred?
There it is!"

Memorial Church was full of tablets to the
memory of those who lost their lives in the mutiny; and lest some should come as sight-seers
rather than worshipers, a quaint notice had been
placed at the entrance: "Whoever thou art that
enterest this church, leave it not without one
prayer to God for thyself, for those who minister,
and those who worship here."

The last quarter of the hour found them under the widespreading tree which still shelters a little Hindoo temple at " Massacre Ghat !" The river looked so quiet and peaceful that, like all other visitors, they found it difficult to imagine the firing of guns and the cries of the wounded which had once echoed over its surface. " It was just here that the English embarked under promise of safe conduct to Allahabad ; but no sooner were their boats out in the middle of the river than they were fired upon by Sepoys from the shore, and all who were not killed were brought back for confinement and final massacre at the well," explained the historian of the party.

The next morning, though it was Sunday, their thoughts were again turned to the mutiny.

Of the many soldiers stationed at Cawnpore, fully three hundred were Nonconformists to the Church of England ; so these had special parade service of their own. This service was in charge at the time of one of the Methodist missionaries, who gave Mother Nind and the little missionary a cordial invitation to be present. The soldiers belonged to the Highland Light Infantry, often spoken of as the " crack regiment " of India, and presented a fine appearance as they marched into church in plaids and kilts. Their guns made a great clattering, as they were deposited in the pews, each at its owner's right hand, in readiness for instant service. This was a lesson learned through the mutiny, as the first attack made by the rebels was on soldiers who were attending church without their guns, at Meerut. Their own band furnished music for them; and they all sang as only a lifetime of Church-going could make them sing. In the evening those who were off duty were free to go to church where they pleased; so many of them were in the habit of following their morning preacher to his own church. This gave Mother Nind an opportunity of talking to them; and remembering her own husband's life as a soldier, she spoke impressively from a heart full of sympathy and love.

New-Year's eve, they were in Lucknow, watching the "first missionary" prepare the dining-room for a watch-night service. This time she had the Hindustani Christians, with a few missionaries, while the English Christians met elsewhere.

On New-Year's day the Sunday-schools, native and English, had their annual Christmas fête together. A large tent had been erected in the park, with benches at one end for the English school and a platform for the speakers. The various native schools came marching into the park, each headed by a band of music and bearing aloft a distinguishing banner. They were seated on the ground facing the speakers, and the English school in groups, still marked by the banners. It was a great company, and not a woman or even a little girl among them. They ranged from small boys to grown men, and numbered many more Hindoos and Mohammedans than Christians; but all were

faithful students of the Bible, and had come to receive prizes for good standing in the annual examination. Before the prizes were distributed, not
only were speeches made to them, but each school
contributed something to the exercises in the way
of readings, or recitations, or songs, until the
whole audience grew a little weary. Then the
"grand old man" stepped to the front, and asked
them "hit and miss" questions on the Sunday-
school lessons of the year. At once every face
grew bright and animated, and the answers poured
forth as volubly and readily as the questions. The
prizes, of which one school received fifty, were
books and bottles of ink for the older ones, and
toys for the younger. The last awards were a few
pice to each one, that he might buy his own refreshments; for, while these curious believers in
caste could study the foreigner's Bible and receive
gifts from his hands, they did not like to have him
touch their food. While the English children were
still partaking of sandwiches, cakes, and coffee, the
Indians had satisfied their simple desires, and were
enjoying the swing of Ferris wheels and merry-go-
rounds, their black eyes sparkling with fun, and
their voices mingling strange calls and shouts with
peals of laughter.

Two days later, another tent was erected in a se-
cluded place on Mission grounds, and our travelers
were invited to a *tamasha* (festival) for women and
girls. It was a true zenana party, not a man or
boy admitted. In all her travels in the East,

18

Mother Nind had not seen before such a brilliant array of jewels and bright colors, orange, red, and purple predominating. How she wished her grand-children could see the pretty sight! As at the other *tamasha*, a table in front was loaded with prizes; for these, also, had been through examina-tions.

They sang and recited the various passages of Scripture which they had laboriously committed during the year, but showed in every move how little they knew of public gatherings and the order to be observed therein. As soon as the exercises were finished and all the prizes of bright, brass drinking-cups and new *chuddars* (veils or shawls required to be worn over the head or shoulders) bestowed, they filed slowly out of the tent, each re-ceiving at the entrance, from native hands, a pack-age of *mithai* (native sweets) wrapped in a leaf.

While these January days were bright and sunny, making outdoor life agreeable, there was a decided chilliness in the air, morning and evening, within the thick walls of the woman's college, built purposely to exclude the heat. How the young missionary, fresh from the steam-heated houses of America, shivered as she came to six o'clock *choti hazri* in the great dining-room, with a thick cape about her shoulders! And, immediately after, she chose the sunniest corner of the veranda for her daily lesson from her Hindustani *padre* (teacher).

"You wouldn't mind the cold if you would take a shower-bath every morning," one of the older missionaries said to her. "After my bath and a run in the yard, it does n't seem a bit cold to me."

Early each morning the *bhesti* (water-carrier) made a tour of the bath-rooms, filling the jars with fresh water from his huge leather bag, which, when distended, made a perfect image of the animal that it once covered. This freshly-drawn water made a pleasant, invigorating shower; but O, the chill that came from using water that had stood in the jar all night!

Even at the "big breakfast" hour the air out of the sun was cold; and the food, which had such long journeys to take from an outside kitchen, was kept warm by means of double plates, with a reservoir in the lower part for hot water.

In the evening all were glad to sit close to the cheery blaze in the drawing-room grate. As they sat there after dinner one night, apparently off duty, the little missionary was emboldened to ask a favor. "I bought a *sari* in Jubbulpur, thinking that I could use it for a sheet while I am in India, and when I get home have it for an Indian costume. Will some one please show me how to put it on?" One of the teachers quickly stepped forward and undertook to drape the long white sheet, whose one bit of color was an orange stripe in the border; but came out with two or three yards left over. She tried again; then some one else tried. "There are so many different kinds of *sari*," they said, in explanation of their failure. "This is much longer than the Bengali *sari ;* and the *chud-dar*, of course, is worn here." So the little missionary put away the *sari*, concluding that the Indian dress, if "only a strip of cloth," was not, after all, so simple a costume as it seemed.

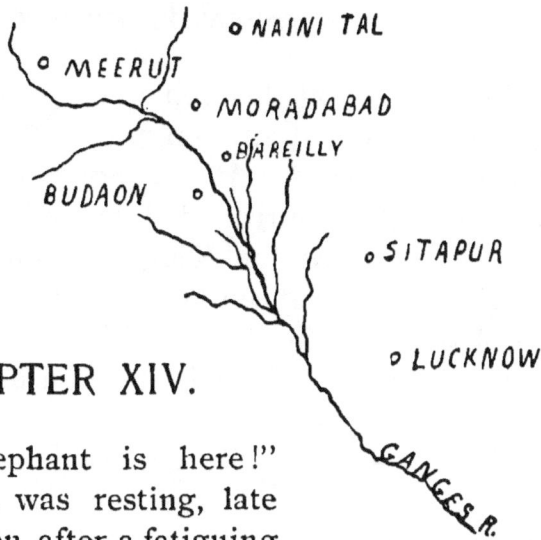

o NAINI TAL

o MEERUT

o MORADABAD

o BAREILLY

BUDAON o

o SITAPUR

o LUCKNOW

GANGES R.

CHAPTER XIV.

"THE elephant is here!"
Mother Nind was resting, late
in the afternoon, after a fatiguing
day, and she hesitated to exchange her comfortable
bed for an elephant's back. But one of the missionaries was waiting in the veranda with her camera; so,
quickly dressing, she was out, entering into the fun
with the youngest and gayest. The elephant was
kneeling to bring the ladder, which was suspended
from his back, within a step of the ground. All
who were going to ride were told to "hurry up, as
it makes him cross to kneel long." When they
were in their places—three on one side and two on
the other—the command was given to the great
creature to rise. This caused some screaming on
top, as the riders slid about the *howdah*, and clutched
each other in the vain effort to keep their places.
But as soon as he was well up, equilibrium was
restored, and they were ready for the picture.
Then, with slow, heavy tread, he moved down the
road, through the college grounds and out into the
city streets. His driver was a turbaned, half-naked

277

coolie, who sat on the elephant's head, guiding him with his toes, and an iron prod, which seemed to answer for a whip. At last they entered an extensive courtyard, surrounded by buildings. "This was the palace of the King of Oude," said one of the riders. "That building near the center was the place where he received his wives (he had four hundred in all). Now it is often used for Christian gatherings."

On the elephant strode, each long, slow step taking them over the ground as rapidly as the swifter pace of many a smaller animal. It stopped in front of the Deaconess Home, and knelt again to let them off. The Deaconess Home was the house in the tomb, where Mother Nind had eaten her Christmas dinner. She wanted to go over the house and see the additions that had been built in the rear for native dormitories. Very simple they were, each with its low *charpoi*, and a place in the stones outside where the occupants could do their own cooking! Though there were few native women as yet who could be trained into deaconesses, there were many who needed a home—the tried and tempted; the afflicted and distressed; the poor and those who had been driven from their houses for Jesus' sake. As they walked down the long veranda, the matron paused before one of these—a poor, blind paralytic—and remarked: "That woman said such a sweet thing the other day. It was this: 'When I open my eyes in heaven, the first thing I shall see will be Jesus.'"

It was growing dark; still Mother Nind lingered to say a few cheering words to her before passing on to other duties.

Everywhere she went there was so much to see and say that, she remarked to the "grand old man" one day, she could find no time to answer her letters.

"Let me send a student from our class in type-writing and stenography at the boys' college to help you," he said. "I know one very well, as he is our cook's son."

He came the next morning. It took only two hours to dictate answers to the bundle of letters that troubled her so; and at night the big bundle was replaced by a pile of carefully executed, typewritten pages. This gave her a little leisure for her neglected note-book. "I can not recall the text of the bishop's sermon at Jubbulpur. What do you suppose it was?" she said to his sister, as she mentioned some of the illustrations.

"O, James has many texts," she replied; "but it's all one sermon."

The little missionary looked up in surprise. A bishop and only one sermon! "How unjust sisters always are!" she thought. But she did not know, the "little bishop of India" did not understand, the secrets of his leadership. Later she learned that there is nothing to inspire the general himself and every soldier in the line, like the cry, "The commander-in-chief is with us!" and she understood why he should weave in and out of every sermon

the thought of Immanuel, until his hearers knew
full well what was coming; yet the more they heard
the more they were thrilled and spurred on to victory.

In her first drive about Lucknow, nothing had
been pointed out to Mother Nind with greater
pride than "Our Methodist Publishing-house." It
was a two-story building, free from debt, and she
agreed with the missionaries that it was a great
achievement. But she understood it better when
she went inside, and saw its presses busily engaged
in turning off religious literature in two strange
languages. A Sunday-school paper was taken from
one of them, and handed to her. It was printed in
Hindi, each character curiously marked at the top
by a straight, horizontal bar. " We can not make
the Urdu character into type at all, it contains so
many dots and broken circles. That has to be
lithographed," her guide explained, as he took her
on to show her some of the work. She thought of
the other publishing-houses she had seen; and
chief among them that of her son-in-law in Foochow. On that last morning he had taken her over
the establishment, and shown her every phase of
the work; but nothing had interested her like the
great cases of type, made to accommodate the
thousands of characters contained in the Chinese
alphabet. The characters most used were placed
near together; still the typesetter had to make
many a journey up and down, in front of his long
case, searching for all that were needed in a given

page. And here in Lucknow was a character so curious that it could not be put in type at all! How easy the home printer's work seemed now, with only twenty-six letters to manipulate!

Much to her regret, she had to leave Lucknow before the beginning of the new term at the Woman's College. She had wanted to see the workings of this experiment to bring an advanced education within reach of the women in India. It was fitting that it should be the inspiration of their "first missionary;" but how sorry she was that the burden of so many first things should fall upon her!

A new building, containing chapel and dormitories for the collegiate department, was approaching completion. "It is costing so much more than I had any reason to expect," she confided to Mother Nind, "that I fear I shall be just where I have always told our younger missionaries never to get—in debt! I am beginning to feel burdened by the prospect."

Many such a tale of anxiety and care had been poured into Mother Nind's sympathizing ears, and there were many yet for her to hear. Often at night the responsibilities carried by her missionary daughters weighed upon her until sleep became a servant that would not hasten at her bidding. Letters multiplied, appeals grew more forcible, and her busy brain was ever cogitating plans to relieve the constant pressure for more workers and more money.

A Sitapur missionary was in Lucknow, to bear
her away for the few days that intervened before
the opening of the North India Conference at
Bareilly. "I like that," said Mother Nind, as she
saw her new hostess selecting tracts to give to
people at the railway stations along the way. At
one station, they met a native pastor who had come
to see Mother Nind for the few moments while the
train waited, and to send a message through her to
the dearly-loved missionary in America who had
been the means of his conversion.

There were two native schools in Sitapur, one
for boys and the other for girls. Though they
were quite a distance apart, until a church could be
built the girls were all marched to the boys' school
for one Sunday service, and the boys to the girls'
school for the other.

The Government was building a church, which
will soon be completed; but as that was intended
only for English soldiers, the missionaries were
busy also putting up a Butler chapel for the native
Christians. Mother Nind well remembered Dr.
Butler's first pleas for the fund, which was now on
interest, aiding in the erection of chapels all over
India; and the sight of each one thrilled her like
meeting with a friend whom she had loved in
former years.

The bread she had cast upon waters all seemed
coming back. Her host reminded her one day of
a debt of gratitude which he personally owed to
her. He was in the home-land on furlough, pre-

paring to return to India. Mission funds were so
low that he had secured his passage with only
steerage accommodations. But Mother Nind happened to hear of his plans, and at once said to
some of her friends: "Now, it's too bad to let this
brother go steerage. Let's take up a collection,
and send him first-class."

"And you did take up a collection," he added,
"and sent me off in good shape, giving me letters of
introduction to your friends in England, with whom
I spent three most happy weeks, resting and sight-
seeing."

Though the work in Sitapur seemed yet in its
infancy, it could boast of two auxiliaries of the
Woman's Foreign Missionary Society. The women
of the Church were united in one, and the other
was made up of the older members of the Girls'
School. One morning, long before breakfast, Mother
Nind was invited to meet both auxiliaries in a union
meeting. The secretaries of the two societies sat
at a table in front, each with her book open before
her. As soon as the introductory hymn and prayer
were finished, the older secretary arose to call the
roll of the society. Each member responded by
stepping forward to deposit her monthly offering,
which seldom exceeded two or three pice, on the
table before the secretary.

Then the other secretary followed with her roll-
call. This was a feature of the meeting which
Mother Nind could not fail to applaud, and she was
also much pleased with the singing.

"Who taught these girls to sing so sweetly?" she asked.

"Our best teacher," was the reply. "She is a Eurasian girl, but well educated and very clever. She can teach a class in the main room, and keep all the classes in the adjoining room quiet, easier than a native woman can manage one little class."

Another namesake was added, while she was in Sitapur, to an already long list of Mary C. Ninds. It was the new-born daughter of one of the pastor-teachers, and she was taken to call at the little, low mud house where it lay. Kneeling in the one dark room of the hut (no way of admitting light except through the door), she thanked God that, poor as it was, this Indian babe had been born into a Christian home.

On her last morning in Sitapur, as she was busily writing, she was interrupted by the sound of music, and looked up to see the boys and girls of the two boarding-schools marching toward the house. They had come to make their salaams for her visit; and after singing the popular, stirring *bhajan* "*Jai Prabhu Yishu*," departed.

It was a happy coincidence that led her to Bareilly, the birthplace of Methodist missions in India, for the annual session of its largest and oldest Conference, the one known as the North India Conference. Four years before, it had been divided to form the Northwest Conference; and in that short time it had gained all that had been lost by division. The gain had been entirely in native preachers, as the number of American missionaries was growing less. "They must increase, while we decrease," quoted the bishop, who, in humility, is another John the Baptist, preparing the way for those who shall do the greater works.

He spoke easily to the Conference in both English and Hindustani, doing away with the interpreter, whom Mother Nind had become accustomed to see as the bishop's right-hand man in Conferences farther east. When the roll was called, the ministers were amused to hear one of the native preachers respond to the name "Seneca Falls." "He was supported by a Church at Seneca Falls, and so he was given that name," explained a missionary from that locality. Then she pointed out Joel Janvier, grown blind and old, but forever honored as Dr. Butler's devoted helper at the time of the mutiny, and the first native preacher of the Methodist Church in India.

Mother Nind was in "the place of her first love." Nearly twenty-five years before, one of the first group of girls adopted in the Bareilly Orphanage had been given her name, and it was here where the first medical missionary of her Society had appealed to a native prince for land upon which to build a hospital. It made her happy to go through this hospital, and think of all the neglected women to whom it had brought healing and comfort. In the waiting-room she saw a low stool and a few books. They were printed in raised characters for the blind; for the native Bible-reader, who sat there

every day, lifted sightless eyes to the waiting patients, and taught them only through the touch of
her skilled fingers.

The orphanage contained over two hundred
girls. Some were growing into womanhood with
a steady, reliable air, which only years of training
could produce; others looked so wild and restless,
it was easy to believe that they had just been
brought in from wretched village homes. Many
were yet babies, laughing and crying by turns, as
they rolled on the ground or were carried on the
shoulders of the older girls. Mother Nind had seen
many quaint babies since she began her travels in
the East, and many quaint ways of carrying them.
First came the almond-eyed baby, strapped tightly
on the back of an older child, its little head dangling in the sun; then the black, naked child of the
Equator, astride it's mother's hips; and now these
dimpled Indian orphans, on the shoulders of women
renowned for their erect, graceful carriage.

During the best hours of the day, all except
the babies were found in the school-room; and
how different this was from other school-rooms!
In Japan and China, each child had a brush and
an ink-stone, painting his lessons on thin sheets
of paper; while the Indian child dipped a stick,
sharpened like a pen, into a bottle of ink, and
wrote on a wooden slate. In some of the schools
where Mother Nind had been, the pupils had read
from the top down; and in those whose books
were printed in horizontal lines there was a differ-

ence, some reading from left to right, others from right to left.

There were differences, too, in their food and manner of eating. In place of the rice and chopsticks, these children broke off bits from their *chapatis* (large, thin wheaten cakes) with their fingers, dipping them into a kind of soup or gravy. They needed no dining-room, for the open ground or broad verandas furnished them with ample space to sit around on their feet, each with a *chapati* in one hand and a brass plate containing the soup in the other. "I have heard high-class natives argue that there is more refinement in their way of eating with their fingers than in ours of eating with a knife and fork; 'for,' they say, 'we always wash our hands carefully before we eat, so we know they are clean; but you are not so sure about your knife and fork.'"

This explanation came from one who had been in India long enough to cease to regard every feature of its ancient civilization as barbaric; but slowly and surely the truth was being revealed to her that other than Occidental ways and customs may be right and proper, and that those might safely be left untouched in their work.

All the wheat for the *chapatis* was ground at the orphanage. One large room was set apart for the "grinding-room;" and the older girls had their regular hours, when they sat two at a stone, grinding out their daily allowance.

During the vacation, they had taken pains with

the decoration of their simple dormitories. Christmas cards from America covered most of the walls;
and in one dormitory the visitors were pleased to
be suddenly confronted by the smiling face of Mrs.
Bottome.

They had just heard an interesting discussion,
in the Woman's Conference, on the subject of
Christmas boxes.   One missionary from the hills
complained that she had been obliged to pay a
large sum of money to a relay of coolies for bringing
a Christmas box to her from the nearest railway
station in the plains, and then found that it contained only English books and papers, which were
of no use there, as she was engaged in native work.

Another told of the duty she had been obliged
to pay because of high appraisals, even old adver-
tising cards given a commercial value, and rated at
a cent apiece.   She added that many people at
home did not seem to know that freight at sea
was charged according to bulk, not weight; for
they used boxes much larger than necessary, filling in the spaces with waste paper, or even empty
pasteboard boxes.

Mother Nind was astonished to find that the
course of true love, as expressed in Christmas
boxes, should so often, and from so many causes,
fail to run smoothly, and made a careful note of
these points for future use in missionary addresses.

The North India Woman's Conference contained so many members, that the reports of the
year's work were not read at the meetings, only

presented for publication. Some came from distant, lonely stations, with more of self-sacrifice wrapped up in their brief lines than many people dream of through an entire existence. One was from dear Mary Reed, the brave, patient missionary to the lepers of Pithoragarh, whose own taint of leprosy acquired in work elsewhere had led her to this special field and separated her entirely from other workers. Her pen seemed dipped in tears, not on her own account, but for the enemy who had been busy sowing tares in her little field, endeavoring to bring even this work to naught.

Dr. Sheldon, working on the distant borders of Thibet, was another member who could not be present, but, by absence, proved her love and devotion.

One morning, Mother Nind went early to the home where the daily sessions of the Conference were held, to see the school that was taught on the back veranda. It was a school for women, wives of the native preachers who belonged to the Bareilly training class. A small part of the Compound was set off for the use of these preachers and their wives; and there they lived simply, as in their own homes, while they studied and prepared for their future work.

The closing day of the Conference came. The Woman's Conference had already adjourned, and its members were seated with the preachers and other missionaries, waiting to hear the appointments. The Finance Committee had been hard at work through the busy six days' session, trying to make the appropriations fit the work (they could not consent to fit the work to the appropriations); but had only failure to report. It was an exigency that required unusual and adroit management; and where could it receive this better than at the hands of the little bishop! In the same matter-of-fact tone in which he announced the usual appointments, he declared six of the missionaries of the Conference who were on furlough, some about to leave, others to return, to be effective at home, thus depriving them of their connection with the Conference, and saving their salaries to apply to native work.

"The people at home can not see our native preachers and their work," he argued. "But they can see the missionaries; and if they find there is not enough money to send them back, they may be aroused to give us what we need."

The following day, Mother Nind packed her belongings again, and started out on a novel journey. After two or three hours of railway travel, she was seated in a *tonga* (a two-wheeled vehicle, with a white top or hood, its two seats arranged back to back), and driven over a steep, winding road, so taxing to the horses that they had to be changed every four miles. A heavy iron harness, however, gave the driver such a sense of security that he drove as furiously, Mother Nind declared, as his famous predecessor in the days of Elisha. But at last they came to a place where the strongest

CHURCH AT MEERUT.
Meeting-place of Northwest Conference.

harness and the most furious driving were of no avail. There Mother Nind was transferred to the curious, boat-shaped *dandi*, and borne on the shoulders of six men the remaining three miles of the journey to Naini Tal.

Years before, she had known of Naini Tal as Dr. Butler's place of refuge during the days of the rebellion. She remembered the sheep-house which he converted into a temporary meeting-place, and thus became the first Methodist Church in India. In later years a sanitarium was erected here for all the missionaries, who, exhausted by the heat of the plains, needed the tonic of its bracing mountain air. And gradually there had grown up, also, a large flourishing school for English-speaking girls. Though started and maintained by representatives of the Woman's Foreign Missionary Society, Government grants and tuitions of the better class students had rendered it quite independent. Its fine buildings, beautiful garden, various departments of work, with a separate hall for music, ten pianos, and a music-teacher fresh from America, made it a not unworthy namesake of the more famous Wellesley College for American women.

And such a setting as it had! All the buildings in Naini Tal were ranged in a semicircle on the mountain-side, step above step, terrace above terrace, and, beyond all, the snowy peaks of the Himalayas, while beneath lay a charming little lake, reflecting more constant, beautiful pictures

than the fairest lady's mirror.   Mother Nind had
seen many a snow-capped mountain, many a crystal
lake.   She had seen them together, and had often
admired the glistening majesty of the one, and the
transparent peace of the other.   But when she had
gazed above, and below, and around, at Naini Tal,
other beautiful scenes faded by comparison, and
she gave to this her highest praise.   " The most
lovely spot on earth," she called it; and, when she
came down from "Snow Seat," where she had gone
for a better view of the heights, she might have
added, " most heavenly;" for she felt like one who
had seen a vision of angels.

A *dandi* carried her all the way down the
mountain to the railway station, and she was soon
back in Bareilly, ready for another trip.   What
contrasts there were in mission work and surroundings!   Now she was to visit a little lone missionary engaged in native work, and situated much like
the other little missionary whom she had visited
in Hirosaki.   On the journey to Bubaon, made
partly by rail, and partly by *tum-tum*, she stopped
at a little place called Aoula.   There, early in the
morning, she was entertained to *choti hazri* in a
native pastor's house.   He had been one of the fortunate preachers who had found their wives in the
Bareilly Orphanage; and his home, though very
poor, was spotlessly neat and clean.   That evening
in Budaon she attended a meeting in one of the
mohullas (wards), occupied by the low-caste sweepers, which helped her to understand what one of

PHEBE ROWE AND HER TENT.

the missionaries had said at a Conference prayer-meeting. His hair was white, and his voice trembled as he told the younger missionaries his experience :

" I came to India, ambitious to study Eastern religions, and to become famed for my ability to dispute their subtle philosophies ; but gradually I have dropped a little lower and a little nearer the Master, until now I am content to be called the ' Sweepers' *Padre.*' "

They did seem the lowest of the low. Children at play with mud-pies were infinitely cleaner than they ; and their minds were so dull and apathetic that they could scarcely grasp the simplest teaching.

Sunday brought Mother Nind the pleasure of preaching in a Butler chapel. There were several of these chapels in Budaon District, she learned ; but as the district contained seven thousand square miles, she thought there could not be too many.

From Budaon she traveled in a *palli gari* (ox-cart) to Moradabad. It was the last of January ; still she was in time to see Christmas presents distributed at the girls' school.

At a prayer-meeting, which had an attendance of three hundred, she was impressed most of all with the dignity and fine presence of her interpreter. What was her surprise to learn that he, who was head master of the Boys' School, and an earnest student of Greek and Hebrew, with a wife at the head of the Dufferin Hospital, had belonged to the despised sweepers' caste !

At a woman's meeting, her attention was called to an old woman, who sat with her children and grandchildren about her. Three generations of Christians they represented. What joy to see such a sight in a heathen land!

The most interesting meeting she attended, however, was in a weavers' *mohulla.* When she arrived at the *mohulla,* she found a mission day-school in session under a widespreading tree in the open air. The mission inspector was present, and sat with his children in front, while the women, still engaged in spinning, gathered in the rear. Many of them had their babies with them, on their hips or at their breasts; and occasionally a man would slip in to form a part of this strange gathering.

But while she lingered in Moradabad, the Northwest Conference, which she had planned to attend, was opening at Meerut. This made her a late arrival, though even then she was a few hours earlier than the little missionary, who had been up in the Punjab, visiting old school-friends.

"You have missed so much," every one said. "You ought to have been here to the self-support anniversary. Bishop W. was here, and said it was the most encouraging feature he had seen in all his tour of Eastern missions.

"Why, what did the people bring?" asked the little missionary.

"O, *everything*, even to pigs' bristles," was the reply.

Later, a native presiding elder, whose wife was a Mary C. Nind from the Bareilly Orphanage, showed the first Mary C. Nind his annual report, neatly written in English. This contained a list of the offerings toward self-support on his district. Besides rupees, annas, pice, and *kauris* (small shells used for money), there were gifts of " flour, grain, dry bread, red pepper, fowls, eggs, pigs, ponies, pigeons, goats, buffalo-calves, lambs, cow-calves, pieces of cloth, wicker baskets, winnowing fans, iron sieves, brooms, coats, earthen cups, and caps."

He not only showed his report, but he introduced her to his children, and brought out his training class of pastor teachers for her inspection. Through an interpreter she asked them questions about their conversion ; and how pleased she was to have answers promptly interpreted to her, that would have graced any class-meeting in America !

CHAPTER XV.

"I SHOULD like to hear 'Jesus knows' once more, as Phebe Rowe sang it in America." This was a request made by Mother Nind during a pause in the first meeting she attended of the Woman's Conference at Meerut.

Phebe Rowe belonged to another despised class, whose mixed blood makes it abhorred of both the nations from which it springs. It is related of her that when she was first admitted to a mission school she seemed so awkward and dull that one teacher in despair remarked to another, "Whatever can we make of *her?*" But the Lord had something he could make of her; for he had already given to this tall, overgrown girl a more precious birth-

300

right than that of rank or position—the gift of a
sweet, beautiful voice.

Through the mission school she had been led
to a consecration as deep and pure and perfect as
that of Frances Ridley Havergal herself; and now
no missionary, from bishop down, was more "meet
for the Master's use" than she.

During the Conference she occupied her own
little tent, living by herself in the same simple
way as when engaged in village work. Soon after
the close, her tent, bed, and cooking utensils were
loaded on a bullock-cart, and started off. Another
bullock-cart was ready to carry herself, three native Bible-women, and a missionary from the South
who, under recent appointment to evangelistic work,
had come North "to see how Phebe did it."
Mother Nind and the little missionary accompanied them to their first village. The little missionary thought the bullock-cart did not bump any
more than the *basha*. "O, it goes well here," they
said, "for these are *puckah* (properly made) roads.
It's when we get off on the *kutchah* (rude or im-
perfect) roads, that we have our hard time." They
had gone only a few miles when they came to a
large village, which contained not one Christian
hearer or inquirer. Curiosity, however, brought
the people running to meet them, some with hands
covered with flour, others with manure, according
to the occupations in which they had been engaged. Phebe and her companions went through
the village, taking advantage of open spaces to

stop and sing and talk to the gathering crowd. If there was n't space enough below, some of the hearers climbed to the housetops and looked down, like Zaccheus of old. At the close of each little meeting, tracts and hymnals were offered for sale.

"Why do n't you give away your tracts?" the little missionary asked.

"Because, if we did, they would soak them into pulp and make baskets of them," replied the missionary from the South.

The visitors were followed to a large pepil-tree outside the village, where they took their stand for a parting song and word of exhortation. They were urged to stay longer, one man inviting them to his house for a drink of milk. But the *Mem Sahib* (Mother Nind) was tired, they said, and must go home to rest. Hearing this, the villagers said no more about their staying; but, on the contrary, politely urged them to go.

"We are not always treated in this way," Miss Rowe had told Mother Nind. "Sometimes we are not allowed in the village at all, but are driven away to our cart or tent, where those who wish to hear must come by night secretly to inquire the way of life." Then they parted, Mother Nind and the little missionary hearing nothing more of the noble evangelist, until in Muttra a letter came, telling of her narrow escape from a tiger. She was walking directly toward him, she wrote, and would not have turned in time, had not the others in the cart noticed her danger and screamed to her to return.

The *Mem Sahib* was tired, and readily accepted
an invitation to remain in Meerut for a week's rest.
One morning, just as she had laid out a pile of letters to be answered, her quick ear caught the sound
of firing. It grew so loud and constant that she
finally put away the letters, got out her big pith
hat and covered umbrella, and started off, saying
to the little missionary, "I must see what is going
on." The latter followed, and soon they were in
the midst of an exciting scene. Soldiers were running here and there across the fields; squads of
cavalry now and then dashed down the road; the
firing was rapid, and seemed to be all about them.
Meeting at last an officer riding slowly and alone,
they ventured to ask, "What does all this mean?"

"It's a sham battle," he replied. "We are pre-
tending to defend the treasury against an attack of
the enemy."

If it had been a real battle, neither he nor any
other officer or soldier could have seemed more in
earnest, been more dignified or alert.

"What an impression such displays as these
must make upon the natives! I don't believe
there 'll be another mutiny," confidently asserted
the little missionary on the way home.

But another morning she was herself attacked
by a whole army of rebels on wings. Unexpectedly
she had walked into a swarm of hornets; and before she could defend herself, they had left their
stings in face, hair, neck, and hands, so many of
them, that the kind friends who gathered about

her shook their heads in alarm at possible results. But the lotion of chalk and vinegar, which they hastened to apply, relieved the pain; and she was ready to laugh when Mother Nind brought out her Bible and read how God used hornets to drive the enemies of Israel from the land of Canaan.

The nice new building in which the Conference had been held, sheltered also a girls' school. There were so many little ones that they were grouped in twos, each little group in charge of an older girl. Saturday was their busy day, when, instead of scrubbing the floors of their dormitories with soap and water, like many other school-girls, they freshened them by applying, with their fingers, a new coat of mud and plaster. This greatly impressed the little missionary; but Mother Nind had seen it before in the native school for girls in Cawnpore. "There they made their own walks, too," she said.

The little missionary sighed. How did she happen to miss that! O, she remembered! That was the day she joined a party that were going down the river alligator-shooting. That was interesting, too, though the part she enjoyed most was seeing *dhobis* (washermen) in groups along the shore, beating their clothes on stones in the river, some of them grooved like real washboards.

Sunday afternoon there were two Epworth Leagues in session at the same time. After the little missionary had seen the Juniors take up their collection, which consisted not only of *kauris*, but of marbles, buttons, and any little thing to which a market value could be attached, she slipped into the Senior League meeting. Mother Nind was in the altar, surrounded by twenty-nine young people in turbans and *chuddars,* each praying aloud for forgiveness of sin and the blessing of a new heart. One of them had been detected a few days before in an apparently would-be robbery; and the others were no doubt in as great need of something more than a mere profession of Christianity.

"We are not satisfied to reclaim them from idolatry and baptize them as Christians; but, just as fast as we can, we try to lead them to a real heart-experience, that shows itself in a changed life." These words came from a missionary's wife, who ably seconded him in his double work among backsliding soldiers and native Christians, young and untried in the faith.

The one week of rest soon came to an end, and our travelers were again whizzing over a hot, dusty Indian railway.

"Will you please permit my brother to come in here?" It was a native gentleman, in European dress, who spoke.

"Yes, if he will not smoke," was Mother Nind's prompt reply.

At this, the brother timidly entered the compartment, and took a seat in the corner opposite them. They rode together until a change of cars put them into a compartment partly filled with native women. One of them wore the Mohammedan *bourka* (a white garment made to conceal the entire person, with tiny bits of lace sewed in over the eyes). As the train started, they were pleased to see the *bourka* drop, and the woman inside, now out of sight of any man, allow herself a little freedom and fresh air.

There was a great fair in progress at Aligarh, their next stopping-place. A quantity of horses stood in rows, with their hind feet tied to stakes in the ground, waiting for purchasers. Not far away, the white tents of " Cook's Circus " gleamed in the sunshine. A few booths contained the real fair, which was an exhibit of cloths, earrings, brass-work, and pottery; and leading to these were rows of shops, some filled with brass drinking-cups and plates; some, again, gay with bright-colored prints; others presenting a tempting display of *mithai*.

In one of the shops sat a little boy whose face was blossomed out with small-pox and black with flies; yet none of the crowd seemed to mind.

The fair was next the Mission Compound; so the missionaries and their guests could not well escape its sights and sounds. One of the missionaries, with his native helpers, made repeated excursions into the crowd, for the sake of distributing tracts and improving any opportunity that offered of talking to the people; and over the Mission Compound, above all other sounds, there rang out each day the Arthur Potts memorial bell, calling Christian girls to their class-rooms, to their Epworth League prayer-meeting, to Sunday-school, and to public worship.

As Mother Nind traveled through the East, her whole course had seemed strewn with memorials—memorial schools, memorial churches, memorial halls, memorial institutes; but among them all, there was not one that appealed to her like this little bell in Aligarh, given in memory of one child, but representing the love of others and the grief of many a Rachel.

In each mission station she visited there were always two tours for her to make. One was a tour of the schools, the churches, the hospitals, that she might have a glimpse of the aggressive work that had been undertaken; the other was a trip to the temples and bathing-places, the homes and haunts of the people, that she might understand the nature of the opposing forces. One of the enemy's strongholds in Aligarh was a Mohammedan college, containing five or six hundred students. The work seemed going on much as in other colleges; the rooms of the students looked quite as neat and orderly as those of any students; and two large classes in the courtyard engaged, one in calisthenics, and the other in a military drill, showed that physical training was not neglected. But a mosque, in course of erection on the campus, led the visitors to ask some questions about the religious element in the curriculum.

"How many times a day do the students say their prayers?"

"They ought to say them five times a day, but many are too busy."

This from a student who felt a little indebted to the missionaries for his knowledge of English.

A little more questioning, and he replied:

"If they do not say them twice a day, they are fined."

From the college to a mosque in another part of the city! The steps were covered with filthy beggars, who go about from place to place like a band of gypsies, and form one of the most repulsive castes in India.

"What a good advertisement for heathenism!" suggested Mother Nind. "That's just what it does for them!"

It was not the hour of prayers; so the praying places, marked out in the pavement in front of the "holy niche," were all unoccupied.

The next place visited was a Hindoo temple. They did not want to take off their shoes; so could only stand at the door and look in. Most of the worshipers seemed to be women. Seated behind a bamboo *purdah* (curtain or screen), they were reciting, after the priests, portions of the Shastras. The idol above them was black, representing Parasnath, the god of wealth.

Across the road from the temple was the home of one of the city officials.

"Those images in the wall around his grounds are all idols," they were told.

Monkeys were climbing over the walls and up the trees; and among the passers-by were men who wore a strangely repulsive look because of signs in colors that had been smeared on their foreheads by the priests, as an evidence of their holiness.

"It's the mark of the *beast* in their foreheads," indignantly exclaimed Mother Nind.

A railroad journey of three hours brought them with a jerk, which was the usual announcement of a station, in front of an unusual view. The peaceful waters of the broad Jumna lay before them; and rising from the opposite shore in shining white terraces were the square, flat-roofed houses of Muttra, their regularity harmoniously broken by the domes and towers of numerous mosques and temples. Close to the river, at intervals, were broad flights of steps, marking the bathing ghats, where the people not only perform their religious ablutions, but stand to feed the "sacred" turtles of the river, and at evening time set out rows of little tapers to light the spirits of the dead down the "holy" stream.

A *gari*, whose every wheel and shutter rattled more than those of any *gari* they had yet tried, carried them over smooth, English-made roads to another Deaconess Home. Its superintendent had recently received a large inheritance, which was already as fully consecrated to the cause of Indian missions as she had ever been. Through her liberality, one overworked missionary had a stenographer to assist her; another, who was compelled to do much traveling over bad roads, received a comfortable carriage; several missionaries were made independent of the Missionary Society for their support, and the work all about was eased and lightened. She herself, however, lived and dressed as simply as the poorest teacher or boarder in the Home, and would have been the last one to murmur over coarse bread, or a poor quality of meat, or the monotony of always wearing the same gown.

Of the many branches of work radiating from the Deaconess Home, Mother Nind and the little missionary thought that they would like to try zenana-visiting. In the same rattling *gari* that brought them from the station, they drove with one of the workers into the city, and along its streets, until she said, " We 'll leave the *gari* here, and walk the rest of the way." Climbing a steep hill, they came to a home of the wealthier class, and asked for admittance. It was a regularly-visited zenana, and they were expected on that particular morning; so the door was soon opened, and they were ushered up-stairs. The wife and her mother-in-law were waiting to receive them, the younger woman dressed in a brilliant, rose-colored costume, edged with gold embroidery. Her bare arms were loaded with bracelets and armlets, her ears weighed down with rings, and such heavy anklets fell about her feet that, every time she stepped across the floor, they clanked like a prisoner's chain. She read a little, to show what she had learned in these visits, and brought out a piece of embroidery which also the zenana visitor had taught her to do. It was not finished, and sadly rumpled and soiled; yet, like any child, she wanted to be taught something new. The visitors looked in pity upon this typical Indian woman, a prisoner both in mind and body, and wondered what she would do if she were to be set at liberty. Would she not, like a little bird who has always been caged and knows no other home, come fluttering back to the shelter of her prison bars again?

The next zenana contained more women. They gathered around Mother Nind, and eagerly studied this new face, finally exclaiming, "How white and beautiful she is!" They had all decorated themselves as much as possible with bracelets and anklets, with earrings and nose-jewels, with rings on their fingers and literal bells on their toes. A monkey had coveted and plucked a bright jewel from the nose of one of the women; but by the side of the torn, ugly space thus made, she had triumphantly bored a place for another jewel.

It reminded the little missionary of the first badly-mutilated ear she had seen. A precious stone, as thick as one's finger, had been inserted, and weighed down the ear until it hung in a rough, ragged scallop. She had seen some with so many little holes pierced in the rims of the ears, and such large rings inserted, that they had to be supported by a chain passing over the head. What a contrast they were to her loved Japanese women, whose dress reflected not one metallic gleam, but only the shimmer of soft silks and crapes; and, with the exception of their hair ornaments, wore

not a ring or a pin, or anything that could be
called jewelry!

Two visits quite exhausted Mother Nind, and
she came away inclined to think that this was the
most difficult and trying work which engaged the
hands and hearts and heads of her missionary
daughters.

Muttra was only a few miles from one of the
"sacred" cities of India, which had for a long
time been given a place in their itinerary as a
substitute for Benares, the one more often visited
by tourists. So on the first day, when they were
free from other engagements, they were rattling in
the *gari* to Brindaban.

Notwithstanding all the temples and idols they
had seen, there was a sense of novelty in entering
this city, whose every public building is a temple,
whose homes are the homes of priests or devotees,
and whose one excitement is that of religious fes-
tivals and pilgrimages.

They stopped first at a new temple, which the
Rajah of Jeypore was building as a work of merit.

Millions of rupees had been expended on its
magnificent stone pillars and arches, which rested
upon foundations so deep and strong that they
promised to endure for untold ages. Fine, delicate
carvings had been wrought upon their surface, and
the interior was so grand and free as yet from images and idols, that for a few moments no one
spoke. At last the little missionary broke the
silence by saying, "How pure and beautiful it all

is!" "Yes," said another missionary, "it will do nicely for a Christian church some day. Just knock out the few idols in front, and it will be ready."

As they went about through the corridors and verandas, grasping more and more of the design of the building, Mother Nind's practical mind was filled with admiration for the architect.

"I would like to see him," she said. "How did he ever conceive such a plan as this? It's worthy of any Christian."

Well it would have been for their opinion of Brindaban, if they had gone no further!

They next entered the outer gate of the largest temple in the city, and found themselves in a paved court, surrounding another inclosure. How much it seemed like the temple at Jerusalem, and more when they learned that only Hindoos were allowed to enter the inner court! But there the resemblance ceased; for the towers surmounting all the gateways were covered with idols, hundreds carved on the outside, and, perhaps, hundreds more within.

Walking to the riverside, they could see what were called the footprints of Krishna, and look up at the tree which he climbed one day, carrying with him the clothes of some of the women who were bathing in the river. As the story goes, this great god of the Hindoos required the nude bathers to dance for him under the tree before he would restore the stolen garments.

Many of the houses had a closed, desolate air, as though they were occupied only on *mela* or festival occasions. They stepped for a moment into the gardens surrounding a fine temple, erected by a Lucknow banker. Its twisted pillars, its marble statuary, the foliage and flowers of the garden, were so restful, that they would have liked to go beyond the posted injunction: "Prevention by religion to European or Mohammedan gentleman go further step."

There was one thing more of special interest, however, which they could see. That was a large structure of red sandstone, built in the shape of a cross, and therefore supposed to have been the work of Jesuits. The rear only they found tenanted by idol shrines and priests.

As they were driving out of this curious city of Brindaban, they saw rows of little houses, surmounted along the eaves by piles of brush, put there to keep numerous and thievish monkeys from clambering down and getting inside. One of these houses was, after all, the unique feature of Brindaban; for in this great city, devoted exclusively to Hindoo worship, that alone belonged to Christian missionaries. From one court to another the priests had contested their right to hold property in a "holy city," but only in the end, under an English Government, to be compelled to yield. It was a tiny place; but it made a rest-house for the workers who came from Muttra to visit the zenanas, and to preach in the open air whenever and wherever they could obtain an audience. Just at that time the priests had risen in a body, and vigorously caused all the zenanas in Brindaban to be closed against the visitors.

Mother Nind and the little missionary had heard about this Aligarh, having listened with bated breath and excited interest to the story of the poor, high-caste lady whose husband beat her so cruelly and so often that she determined to run away. Those Christian workers who came from Muttra were so gentle and kind, she would cast herself upon their mercy, she thought. And so one day she presented herself at the Deaconess Home, and told her pitiful tale for the first time to sympathizing ears. How their hearts ached for her at the Home, and how they wanted to help her! But the superintendent was wise and firm. "It would bring us into trouble, and all our work in Muttra and Brindaban to naught, if we should take you in; we can not do it. You must return to your husband." The poor woman pleaded as for her life, and so successfully that she was allowed to remain in the Home that night; but the next day she was sent away. Scarcely had she gone when inquirers appeared at the door in search of her. Meanwhile one of the Bible-women had slipped out, and, in her pity for the hunted creature, had concealed her in her own mother's home, which was not far from the Mission Compound. The superintendent unaware of this, truthfully answered all the questions put to her, saying that the fugitive had been there, but had been sent away. The pursuers went from door to door, until the object of their search realized that she was doomed unless she also moved on. Then from door to door she went, fairly flying in her desire for freedom, until she spied a sweeper's costume. Donning this, she grasped a broom and began to sweep the road, hoping in that disguise to evade pursuit. But her awkwardness betrayed her; she was apprehended and carried back to the waiting husband, angered by her flight and grown more cruel than before; and part of the trouble which the superintendent had feared, came to pass in the temporary closing of the work in Brindaban.

The missionaries in Muttra, as in most of the Indian cities where soldiers were quartered, had one church for English-speaking people, and another for natives. The latter was a memorial church, bearing the name of Flora Hall, and used through the week as a day-school for boys.

In some miraculous way a site for this hall had been secured in the heart of the city. There, with only the image-covered spires of Hindoo temples and the proud domes and minarets of Mohammedan mosques to rise as high as its simple bell-tower, with its shop at its entrance for the manufacture and sale of endless duplicates in brass of the gross, sensual Krishna, it stood even more of a wonder and cause for thankfulness and praise than the little rest-house in Brindaban.

The school for girls was out of the city, con-

nected with the Deaconess Home, and surrounded by
one of the high walls that made a zenana of every
boarding-school in India. It was kept so neat and
clean that when the father of one of the girls came
to see her, she noticed for the first time that he was
dirty; then she began to pray most earnestly, morning and night, "O God, please make my father
clean."

Mother Nind went through the school-grounds,
just as the evening *chapatis* were being baked over
the coals. The cook sat on the stones by her low
fire, dextrously turning the large cakes with her
fingers, over and around, until they were puffed up
light and brown. Not far away was another woman
winnowing the grain in shallow baskets. And the
grindstone was there, too, to turn it into flour;
all the processes of preparing food, except raising the
wheat, done in the school! What simple living!
No wonder that an Indian girl could be supported
for twenty dollars per annum!

CHAPTER XVI.

AGRA
JEYPORE
AJMERE
BAROUA
BOMBAY
POONA

THERE was small-pox in Delhi; so there was
in every Indian city; it was impossible to escape it
anywhere. But the reports that came from Delhi
were more startling than those from any other city;
so that had been dropped from the itinerary. And
Mother Nind was not sorry! She was not fond of
sight-seeing. She loved to talk with the missionaries; to see their growing work; to preach and
sing and pray; to have little chats with the native
preachers and Bible-women; to receive the confi-
dences of young soldier-boys, who, after a wild,
reckless life in and out of the army, had been led
by a cup of tea and the promise of a pleasant, social
hour, into some quiet mission chapel, and finally to
the Savior himself. All these things she enjoyed.
But she wearied of the temples and palaces, the
museums and the gardens, the monuments and
towers; of the work in brass; of the carvings and
embroideries; of all the sights which other travel-

318

ers made their trip around the world on purpose to
see. So, when her hostess in Agra proposed, as
soon as she was settled in his home, to give her a
drive to the Taj, she did not respond as he expected.

" I must rest and prepare for the prayer-meeting
this evening," she said; and then, as if she would
ward off other invitations of a similar nature : "Anyway, we must not take your time for such things,
brother."

But later she relented, remarking, with a twin-
kle in her eye: " I suppose people would think me
too much of a fool if I did not go to see the Taj."

Then she did just what other travelers were wont
to do – got an early start one morning; watched
through the drive for the first appearance of its
white domes and minarets; climbed to the top of
the gateway for a good view of the whole wonderful creation in its dazzling whiteness, and the ma-
jestic avenue of cypress-trees, whose dark, solemn
shadows are reflected from the surface of a long,
narrow reservoir of clear water, and brightened
and beautified by numerous flower-beds; walked
slowly along this avenue until, as she approached
the Taj itself, she was obliged to stop and close her
eyes, for its glory in the morning sun was greater
than she could bear; then around on the shady
side to examine the carving and inlaid-work, and
to admire the simplicity and perfection of every
detail; inside for more carving and finer inlaid-
work, and a few notes of song to hear the wonderful echo; down below to see the real sarcophagi.

of which those above were only copies; to note
that, notwithstanding the glory of this most magnificent tomb ever erected to the memory of a
woman, her sarcophagus was marked with a tablet,
and his with a pen-box, to show that woman was a
blank for man to write upon; to see also that the
hand of the vandal had been at work removing
precious stones and destroying much of the beauty
of the delicate tracery in leaves and flowers; to
wonder again, as they came out, how the whole
of the Koran could be wrought in marble on the
inside and outside of this gem of all architecture;
after she had passed the gate, to stop and buy a
few photographs of one of many eager venders who
pushed their pictures from both sides of the carriage at once into her lap; and then, on her return
to the house, to make more purchases of an equally
eager crowd, who filled the veranda with samples
of inlaid work "just like that on the Taj."

She had really done it all so well and so much
like any other traveler, that her host was emboldened to propose a trip to the fort the next morning.
And where, out of India, could she see a more perfect reflection, in stone, of the pride and vanity, the
power and weakness, the glory and the shame, the
ambition and the fall of an ancient civilization?
Within its extensive walls she found a palace and
a prison. Above were marble audience-chambers,
mirrored bath-rooms, and gardens filled with fountains and flowers; beneath were dungeons. By
the palace rose the domes of the Pearl Mosque,

whose pillars and arches of purest white marble were so exquisitely shaped that at a little distance they looked like one great pearl; and not far away from this ideal place of worship, which would seem to inspire only the noblest thought and feeling, the Great Mogul himself, who built the Taj, had been imprisoned by his own son. Overlooking the river was the piazza where, in his dying hour, as a last favor, he had asked to be brought for another look at the beautiful tomb where he was soon to find rest by the side of his loved wife.

A small guard of English soldiers now formed the only occupants of the fort; fountains no longer played over mosaic pavements, bringing out the brightness and beauty of their coloring; the inlaid ceilings, set with gems and tiny mirrors, were not illuminated now, except for some distinguished visitor like the Prince of Wales; the palace, the mosque, the dungeon, were all deserted.

It was past the middle of February, and still there was a Sunday-school Christmas *fête*, to be made memorable by Mother Nind's presence. The work in Agra was comparatively new, and the Christians who had been gathered together were almost entirely of the sweeper caste. For the first time, in church, she saw men winding their turbans around their heads; and after the *mithai* had been distributed, there was quite a squabble, some lingering for hours about the house in the hope of receiving more. This little incident was an added link in the long chain of observations that showed

21

her how much faith and courage and perseverance
were needed in the struggle to bring up a low-caste
Christian to even a respectable plane of living.
Some of the villages and mohullas she had visited
contained the dirtiest Christians she had ever seen.
They had renounced idolatry and been baptized
into the Christian faith; but for all the rest, how
much patient, devoted, mother-like training they
needed!

The next journey brought her, after an all-
night's ride, to Jeypore, the most prosperous,
purely native city in all India. She and the little
missionary had now become independent travelers.
At first, some one had taken pains to accompany
them from one place to the next; but the latter
felt equal to any emergency, since she had learned
to call out, "Coolie hai!" when they needed to
change cars, and to ask for *"garham pani"* (hot
water), when they were ready for luncheon. Besides, there were English-speaking guards at all the
large stations. There was only one point in which
the two travelers disagreed. The little missionary
wanted to see Mother Nind resting in a comfortable carriage, especially on a night journey. But
Mother Nind was opposed to "needless self-indul-
gence." In all her traveling in America she had
seldom availed herself of the comfort of sleeper
or drawing-room car; so, now in India, she began
to think second-class too good, and, to the little
missionary's dismay, proposed third-class travel
altogether.

Their missionary host in Agra, however, managed the trip to Jeypore, securing seats ahead in a second-class ladies' reserve. There was only one other passenger, a Scotchwoman, who also was bound for Jeypore. She knew more about the city than they, and kindly shared her information, proposing that they go to the same hotel, and hire a carriage together for sight-seeing. Her son was in another compartment. He was a forward youth, and should have been in school; but ill-health had led his mother to take him out, and give him this trip to India. It seemed strange enough to Mother Nind and the little missionary to be going to a hotel. In all their journeyings, they had not once been entertained outside of a mission home; and they were glad, indeed, for the companionship of strangers.

After breakfastig together at the hotel, they were driven to the zoological gardens. "I believe India is the easiest country in the world in which to have zoological gardens," declared the little missionary. "The whole country teems with animal life. Every city has a jungle at its gates, full of wild beasts, poisonous snakes, and beautifully-plumaged birds."

But it was too hot to linger in the gardens, and they were glad to escape to the cool halls and corridors of the Albert Museum, not far away. This building was a great surprise to the visitors—a large, handsome, modern museum, erected by a native prince in honor of the Prince of Wales,

and filled with curios from many lands! Mother
Nind's English heart filled with pride as she looked
at its beautiful colors and arches and wandered
through its great rooms, noting how like it was to
any English or American museum, each distinct
article neatly labeled, and put in its proper case
and department.

The School of Arts was the next place to visit,
the driver of their carriage informed them. This
was another wonderful place, as it gave them an
opportunity to see Indian artisans at work. The
exhibits were similar to much that had been seen
in the museum, and were for sale; but alas for the
degenerate taste, which led the visitors to pass by
all the beautiful work in brass, and bear triumphantly away a souvenir spoon, with a half-rupee hol-
lowed out for the bowl and a monkey sporting on
the handle!

It was time for luncheon; and after that,
Mother Nind felt too tired for more sight-seeing;
so the others went off without her.

The palace of the Maharajah! What an interesting gateway, with such curious pictures all over its
frescoed walls! They were admitted to a few
rooms inside; and as they entered one, the Scotch
lady got out her guide-book, and read: "A large
room, with ceiling decorated in red and gold, used
as an audience-chamber."

Hastily glancing around, she remarked in an
undertone, "But this is n't a large room, and it has
no such ceiling as that."

By this time, they were ushered into another room, again and the guide-book was consulted, with equally unfortunate results.

"What a hard way of seeing the world, to try to corrobate everything in the guide-book!" thought the little missionary.

They were taken to see the Rajah's elephants, and camels, and horses, and carriages, and alligators; but the place of all places in Jeypore they found to be an inclosed square, filled with ancient astronomical instruments in stone. When they saw great sun-dials, such as were used in the days of Hezekiah, and many other curious designs, to which they could give no name, exclamations of delight came rapidly to their lips, and the Scotch lady hurried back to the carriage to call her son. He was comfortably seated reading a novel, and none of her persuasions availed to make him think it worth while to leave the light fiction, which he could read at any time, for that which was real and historic, and only for a moment within his reach. Poor mother! He coughed more than usual that night, and when they met in the morning she had given up her plans for farther sight-seeing in that vicinity, and decided to try another place for him.

Mother Nind and the little missionary were going on also to Ajmere. Here they saw a college built by the chiefs of all the native States of Rajputana for the education of their sons. Each of the young princes had his own home; and as no two of them are alike, and all models of architectural beauty, the campus presented a very pleasing appearance. Mother Nind had missionary friends in Ajmere to take her on her last round of Indian schools and churches, and mosques and temples.

On the long journey to Baroda she began to feel ill. They had started third-class, and as long as they had a reserved compartment they were quite comfortable. But at last they were transferred to a long car, with only two seats at one end reserved for them, and the remainder filled with natives. Night was coming on, and Mother Nind ill in that car, with a beautiful second-class carriage next them entirely empty! The little missionary determined to make a change. Slipping out at one of the stations, she had a few words with the guard, and came back to bear Mother Nind and her luggage with such haste into the next carriage that the latter, for some time, did not know how it had happened. But she forgave the little missionary; for soon after their arrival in Baroda she had to give up entirely, and call herself sick. Fortunately she was in a home with two doctors and a dispensary; and in a few weeks' time she was able to be about again. But the days were growing very warm. Only the early mornings still retained a slight connection with the cool season, and Mother Nind knew she must be careful. "If I can only get to Central Conference, I will ask for nothing more," she said. Her passage from Bombay was engaged for March 21st, and the Conference would be at Poona the week preceding. It would mean ten or twelve extra hours of railroad travel; but the road led through mountain passes, giving her the finest pictures from a car window which she had seen in all her journeyings in India. It was a pleasant change from the vast expanse of dry, dusty plains, which had thus far formed the bulk of the scenery through which she had passed. But it was very hot, and again, in Poona, she was not strong enough to attend many meetings. All the Methodist Conferences in India were represented at this Central Conference, and she saw again many of the missionaries whom she had visited at their work, besides others from Madras, whom she knew only by name.

The most remarkable feature of the Conference was a sermon by the bishop, in which he seemed to his inspired audience like another Moses or Joshua, or one of the prophets, looking into the future with such glorified vision that, with great power, he exhorted his people to "have faith in God." Directly after this sermon his own faith was tested in a very practical way. One of the missionaries came to him and said: " I have two pastor-teachers in my employ, and nothing to pay them. Shall I retain them on faith, or discharge them?"

Pundita Ramabai's school was located in Poona, and one day Mother Nind summoned strength to visit this best known, perhaps, and most interesting of all Indian institutions. The high-caste

Brahmin lady who, by her enterprise and perseverance, founded the school, was very gentle in
her dealings with her widow pupils. She allowed
them to observe caste rules in cooking their food
and in washing their garments, and she did not re-
quire them to attend Bible-classes. Every morning at five o'clock she and a Christian assistant had
prayers and studied the Bible together. Gradually
the pupils, at their own request, had joined this
early class, until fifteen out of the fifty-two in the
school had become Christians. Then, strange to
say, Ramabai was troubled, for the funds she had
raised in America had been contributed to the support of *Hindoo* widows. Would their American
patrons be pleased to support, instead, *Christian*
widows? She wrote at once to know their wishes,
and was greatly relieved when the reply came back,
" No objections!"

The Christians were very anxious to remain,
and had already besought her to allow them to
grind, or do any other hard work by which they
could earn their own support.

The buildings were well furnished and scrupu-
lously clean. One bed in each dormitory was raised
high above all the others. This was for the teacher,
supposedly to give her a more commanding survey
of the room, and elevating her, even in sleep, to a
position above her pupils.

Mother Nind was ill again at the close of the
Conference, and arrived in Bombay only a day or
two before sailing. The little missionary had gone

on ahead, and had much to tell her of all that she had
seen. There had been two weddings—one a Ben-
Israelite wedding, with service all in Hebrew. The
groom wore golden-brown silk trousers, a pink silk
vest, and a round pith hat, with a lace veil thrown
over it during part of the ceremony. The bridal
veil was a dream of loveliness, made of jasmines
and roses.

The other was a double wedding. The brides
were sisters, who had been among the first pupils
in the Methodist Girls' School at Bombay. They
looked very pretty in simple white silk *saris.*

There had been a visit to the silent, open
towers outside the city, where the Parsees deposit
their dead for vultures to feed upon, and the most
interesting and varied zenana-visiting of all had
come just at the close of their India journeyings.

They went first to a Mohammedan home.
After climbing two flights of stairs, they were admitted to a woman's prison apartment. On the
floor at one side was her bed, a simple mattress.
Near by, elevated on a comfortable wire bedstead,
was her husband's bed. She was a believer, and a
woman of considerable intelligence, reading her
own Bible lesson and listening attentively to the
explanation given.

The next zenana contained several Hindoo
women. They sat upon the floor, giving their visitors seats upon the bed. They could not read,
and listened only as children listen to what they
can not understand or appreciate. Their love of

jewelry and childish ways made them seem many
grades below the quiet, intelligent Mohammedan
woman just visited, and many more below the one
next seen. She was a Parsee, daughter of a priest
living on Malabar Hill, the most beautiful quarter
of the city. She was studying both in English and
Urdu, and her teacher believed her to be a real
Christian. Her lesson for the day was in Exodus,
and, after asking many questions that had arisen
in her mind about it, she answered a few regarding
the Parsee religion, showing her visitors the *sacred
cord* around her waist, also the thin, white skirt
worn underneath. "It must be thin and white,"
she said, "so that the heart may be clearly seen.
We do not worship the sun and moon," she added;
"we only stand near, and pray to *God.*"

Two large steamers sailed from Bombay, March
21st. One contained our travelers and many missionaries, including several General Conference
delegates; the other, the bishop, with his family,
and other delegates. A farewell reception had been
given to them the evening before at one of the
Methodist churches of the city; and now they
were sailing away, the hearts of all full of love for
India and faith in her ultimate evangelization.

Among these missionaries were Mr. and Mrs.
Spencer Lewis, of our West China Mission, who,
with their son and daughter, were on their way to
their United States home for needed rest, but *en
route* had visited our missions in China, Burmah,
and India. Mother Nind had known Mrs. Lewis

from her childhood, and it was a great delight to
meet them in Bareilly at the Conference, and travel
with them in India, accompany them from Bombay
to Marseilles, Paris, and London, where they parted,
to meet once more before they sailed to their field
of labor in 1897, leaving their son and daughter
behind for education. These faithful missionaries
know much of Paul's experiences, "In journeyings
often, in perils of waters, in perils of robbers, in
perils by the heathen, in perils in the city, in
perils in the sea, in weariness and painfulness, in
watchings often, in hunger and thirst, in fastings
often," and, as superintendent of our West China
Mission, Brother Lewis can add, "Besides those
things that are without, that which cometh upon
me daily, the care of all the Churches."

Mother Nind and the little missionary were
greatly crowded. They were going second-class,
in a stateroom containing six berths, all of them
occupied. The heat was intense, and Mother Nind
felt so weak and worn that she no longer entertained a shadow of regret of giving up the coveted
trip to Palestine, which she had hoped to make;
but looked forward with increasing longing to the
healthful, invigorating climate of dear old England, and to the society of loved brothers and sisters once more. She had already written to them:
"What does it matter if we are not as handsome,
as blithesome, as toothsome, as we once were!
Our hearts are young and tender and joyous, overflowing with God's love; and though we are near-

ing the end of the journey, the prospect is all radiant with glory. I expect Alfred, the dear, sweet baby of the family (sixty-four years old), will still have the rosy cheeks, the dimples, the benignant smile, the hearty laugh; for he is 'way behind us in the race. Can he run as fast as ever? Well, if he can, he can not overtake us, who got ahead of him at the start. Let us all run with patience the race set before us, looking unto Jesus, the author and finisher of our faith."

As we neared the Gulf of Aden our thoughts turned lovingly to our dear Florence Nickerson, who, January 31, 1887, was called to her heavenly home, and whose mortal remains were buried in the sea where they rest until the "sea gives up the dead that are in it." Our Phebe Rowe, who accompanied her as nurse and companion, continued her journey to the United States, to comfort the bereaved family and bless homes and Churches by her presence and power.

Soon they were in the Red Sea, which, as Mother Nind expressed it, might well be called the Red-hot Sea; then through Suez Canal, and out into the Mediterranean, where it was cooler. Their steamer landed them at Marseilles, a swift railway journey bearing them on to the English Channel. It was a short voyage across, and then she was speeding by rail to Loughton. How cool and refreshing the air of her native land felt against her pale, wasted cheeks! What rest to her eyes in the sight of its leaves, its green hedges, its well-tilled

farms! What joy in her heart at meeting the
brothers and sisters still spared to her!

Every day she could drive or walk with them
over its unrivaled country roads. Every night she
slept sweetly, freed for a while from all anxiety and
care. By the time the travelers arrived from the
trip through the Holy Land, she looked so much
better that the little missionary said she should not
have known her.

Still she staid on! She visited the house where
she was born, and "born again;" saw the room in
which she told her first lie; entered the garden
where she played as a child; visited the schools
which she attended; bought sweets again from the
baker's shop, which was still standing, and looked
just as it did sixty-five years before. She went to
the chapel where she had made her first profession of
faith and became Sabbath-school superintendent;
to the mission where she had taught her first Sabbath-school class; to Exeter Hall in London, where
her childhood missionary zeal was kindled to white
heat, as she listened to Moffatt, Morrison, Williams,
Campbell, James, and others, and where now again
she could listen to missionary speakers from many
fields.

What pleasure it was to attend a deaconess
meeting in City Road Chapel, and hear the reports of
work accomplished in the United Kingdom; to listen to Frances Willard and Lady Henry Somerset,
as they addressed an immense and appreciative audience in Queen's Hall; to enter and to be im-

pressed once more by the grandeur of St. Paul's and the quiet solemnity of Westminster Abbey!

It was also dear to her heart, that the desire often arose with her to remain in England, and live a little longer where her parents lived, die where they died, and be buried with them until the resurrection. It seemed like such a quiet, peaceful ending to her long, active life. But there was another desire paramount to this, the desire to " bear fruit in old age;" and so, after one long, restful, happy summer amid the scenes of her childhood, she bade a final farewell to them all, and departed for the land of her maturer years.

The voyage from Southampton to New York was a notable one. The steamship *St. Louis*, of the American Line, is one of the best, and among its passengers was the distinguished Viceroy Li Hung Chang and his suite. He was genial and courteous to all. The entrance to New York Harbor was a memorable one. Amid the firing of crackers, the booming of cannon, the waving of flags and banners from boats and ships gayly decorated, the *St. Louis* slowly and proudly steamed to the landing, where the corporation of New York was waiting to do honor to the representative of the Celestial Empire. Resting on the Sabbath according to the commandment, a short stay at Clifton Springs, New York, a missionary address, then on to Detroit to " home, sweet home," where loving friends were waiting to welcome friend and mother.

www.ingramcontent.com/pod-product-compliance
Lightning Source LLC
Chambersburg PA
CBHW021123270326
41929CB00009B/1017